WHAT PEOPLE ARE SAYING ABOUT
DIGGING DEEPER

"Rob Eaton's treatment of 'The Pahoran Principle' is fresh and very interesting. It's full of well-written insights and practical applications."

John Bytheway, author and speaker

"Rob Eaton has masterfully woven together Book of Mormon teachings that will inspire and challenge the sincere disciple."

Nathan Williams, professor of Religious Education, BYU–Idaho

"Coming together in Rob Eaton you have a brilliant mind, an accessible manner, a vibrant love for the Book of Mormon, and a great heart, all leading to powerful insights. The experience his students are able to have can now be somewhat replicated through this powerful book."

Greg Palmer, professor of Religious Education, BYU–Idaho

"With just the right mix of application and scripture, Rob Eaton reminds us that the Book of Mormon is full of lessons for everyday living. Beginning and ending with the perspective that 'the crux of the matter is Christ,' Eaton teaches the reader how the Book of Mormon helps us understand and learn from affliction, of the need to flee evil and embrace good, how not to let prosperity divert us from righteousness, and that Satan is real and has an army of allies. I learned from this book and enjoyed its applicability to everyday living."

David Magleby, Dean of the College of Family, Home, and Social Sciences, Brigham Young University

DIGGING
DEEPER

DIGGING DEEPER

Discovering and Applying Life-Changing
Doctrines from the Book of Mormon

ROBERT EATON

DESERET
BOOK

SALT LAKE CITY, UTAH

To my mother,

whose example and teachings

helped me learn to love the scriptures

Library of Congress Cataloging-in-Publication Data

Eaton, Robert
  Digging deeper : discovering and applying life-changing doctrines from the book of Mormon / Robert Eaton.
      p.   cm.
  Includes bibliographical references and index.
  ISBN-10 1-59038-618-3 (hardbound : alk. paper)
  ISBN-13 978-1-59038-618-7 (hardbound : alk. paper)
  1. Book of Mormon—Criticism, interpretation, etc. 2. Christian life—Mormon authors. I. Title.
  BX8627.E22 2006
  289.3'22—dc22   2006010407

Printed in the United States of America
Publishers Printing, Salt Lake City, UT

10   9   8   7   6   5   4   3   2   1

CONTENTS

LESSONS FOR THE CONFLICT

ACKNOWLEDGMENTS

In writing this book, I am grateful for the suggestions and encouragement of many individuals. My wife, Dianne, and my daughter, Rebecca, provided helpful editorial feedback, as did my friends Mark and Kim Beecher, and Kevin Packard. Cory Maxwell at Deseret Book has been remarkably kind, supportive, and insightful throughout the publication process; this book is better book because of his efforts. I also appreciate the encouragement and efforts of Jeff Simpson at Deseret Book, who helped sharpen the focus of this manuscript. Dave Magleby, Greg Palmer, Nate Williams, and John Bytheway provided helpful encouragement along the way as well.

Others at Deseret Book were also very helpful in the publication of *Digging Deeper*. Richard Peterson provided careful editing, Shauna Gibby was the designer who (among other things) provided the nifty graphics that would make the most pedestrian of thoughts seem profound, and Laurie Cook did the typesetting. I appreciate the help of the many other Deseret Book employees whose names I don't know who helped in the production and distribution of this book.

I am particularly grateful for my students. I have benefited immensely from their ideas, some of which undoubtedly have made their way into *Digging Deeper*. Above all, to the extent any of my insights are inspired, I freely acknowledge the Lord as the source of such inspiration. And to the extent any of my statements are uninspired or doctrinally inaccurate, I'm afraid I'm solely responsible for such errors myself.

INTRODUCTION

When he was still relatively new to the Quorum of the Twelve, Elder Dallin H. Oaks humbly submitted a draft of one of his talks to one of his senior brethren for some feedback. His fellow Apostle wrote just two words on the talk, but they were profound: "Therefore, what?"[1] The moral Elder Oaks drew from the story was that his talk was incomplete because he hadn't included a "vital element: what a listener should do."[2] We learn from Elder Jeffrey R. Holland that President Boyd K. Packer often asks that same question after a presentation or exhortation. Even the Savior's "sermons and exhortations were to no avail," observes Elder Holland, "if the actual lives of His disciples did not change."[3]

Gospel scholarship, then, is about more than just getting doctrines into our heads; it's about getting them into our hearts and lives. As Elder Oaks later explained in the context of gospel teaching:

> A gospel teacher is concerned with the results of his or her teaching, and such a teacher will measure the success of teaching and testifying by its impact on the lives of the learners. A gospel teacher will never be satisfied with just delivering a message or preaching a

sermon. A superior gospel teacher wants to assist in the Lord's work to bring eternal life to His children.[4]

Of course, if we simply focus on changing behavior without understanding doctrine, our efforts never seem to have much lasting effect. Thus, President Packer has also repeatedly reminded us that the "study of the doctrines of the gospel will improve behavior quicker than a study of behavior will improve behavior."[5] Simply discussing behavior without understanding doctrine may be like hacking away at the branches of life's problems rather than dealing with the roots.[6] President Packer's teachings remind us that, taken together, we should strive both to understand doctrine *and* to apply it to our lives in order to bring about change.

This book strives to do both. Nephi himself loved to "liken all scriptures unto us, that it might be for our profit and learning" (1 Nephi 19:23). My aim is to emulate Nephi by examining several of my favorite stories and themes in the Book of Mormon with an eye to answering the *therefore, what?* questions of life. My hope is that each chapter helps readers understand the Book of Mormon's doctrines better while simultaneously inspiring them to apply those doctrines in their lives.

By both discussing doctrine and attempting to apply it, this book falls somewhere in between a doctrinal commentary and a devotional or self-help book. While I own and use many wonderful scriptural commentaries, the breadth of their scope necessarily limits the depth of their analysis. Elder Neal A. Maxwell once likened the Book of Mormon to "a vast mansion with gardens, towers, courtyards, and wings." Such a theological estate is fraught with opportunities for exploration, yet "we as Church members sometimes behave like hurried tourists, scarcely venturing beyond the entry hall. . . . There are rooms yet to be entered, with flaming fireplaces waiting to warm us."[7] Because this book does not try to systematically tour every room of this scriptural mansion, we are able to thoroughly explore the rooms we do visit, as it were, spending much more time in them than the typical "hurried tourist" or the author of a comprehensive commentary.

This book is also different from doctrinal commentaries in an even more fundamental way than its more limited scope. While more scholarly works tend to focus solely on helping gospel students understand doctrines, I also discuss the *therefore, what?* questions—something beyond the scope of a more scholarly work. If the charge is writing a book geared toward changing and improving people's lives, I plead guilty. (Incidentally, the Book of Mormon itself is precisely such a book, although this book certainly isn't in its league.)

Yet my attempt to inspire behavioral change is not grounded merely in "the philosophies of men interlaced with a few scriptures and poems," since, as Elder Holland notes, in times of crisis such things "just won't do."[8] (Elder Holland is undoubtedly describing the habits of some gospel teachers who feed their students "theological Twinkies,"[9] not the authors of outstanding LDS literature that is more uplifting than academic.) There's an awful lot of discussion of scriptures and doctrines in this book because President Packer is right: there's really nothing quite like "true doctrine, understood," to change "attitudes and behavior."[10]

In short, this book is an attempt to share my understanding of some of the wonderful doctrines of the Book of Mormon and my answers to the question we should ask ourselves after studying all such doctrines: *Therefore, what?*

LESSONS ON

LIFE'S
JOURNEYS

PREPARED AGAINST THE WINDS AND MOUNTAIN WAVES

Our afflictions can help us sail instead of sink.

In the religion classes I teach, I frequently conduct an informal survey. I ask students to take a moment to write down a season in their life when their prayers were the most intense and effective—a time when they felt particularly close to the Lord. I then ask them to write down the season in their life of their greatest trial. Then I ask how many of them wrote down the same season in their life as a response to both questions. Almost without fail, a majority of students raise their hands.

Such a result is a graphic reminder that the Lord allows us to suffer afflictions—and occasionally sends us trials—because He wants to draw us to Him in a way that prosperity and ease never can. After noting how quick we are to forget the Lord when things are going well, Mormon offers this insight: "And thus we see that except the Lord doth chasten his people with many afflictions . . . they will not remember him" (Helaman 12:3). Perhaps no story in the Book of Mormon more richly and symbolically demonstrates this principle than that of the Jaredites' voyage to their land of promise. From their experience we learn that rather than remove potentially terrifying winds and waves from our lives, the Lord prepares us to be able to withstand them, since they are often what propels us toward our personal lands of promise.

Unfortunately, the winds of affliction do not guarantee spiritual progress. If we do not let the Lord prepare us and lead us, the very winds that might have helped us sail can also cause us to sink. As demonstrated by the Nephites' experience at the end of many years of war, the same afflictions that soften some people's hearts can harden the hearts of others. Whether life's trials make us better or bitter—whether the winds of adversity cause us to sail or sink— hinges on our attitude toward God.

"I PREPARE YOU AGAINST THESE THINGS"

In preparation for his people's voyage to the land of promise, the brother of Jared built eight unusual barges just as the Lord had directed. Anxious about making a mammoth voyage in the dark and with no air, the brother of Jared poured out his concerns to God in prayer. The Lord's answer and the prophet's subsequent smith-work and bold prayer in Ether 3 are well known. However, tucked away in the Lord's initial answer to the brother of Jared is a marvelous lesson:

> For behold, ye shall be as a whale in the midst of the sea; for the mountain waves shall dash upon you. Nevertheless, I will bring you up again out of the depths of the sea; for the winds have gone forth out of my mouth, and also the rains and the floods have I sent forth.
>
> And behold, I prepare you against these things; for ye cannot cross this great deep save I prepare you against the waves of the sea, and the winds which have gone forth, and the floods which shall come (Ether 2:24–25).

The Lord's description of the nautical mayhem that awaited the Jaredites was wonderfully graphic: waves that loomed as large as mountains would come crashing down upon them. Yet His promise was sure: the Master of the elements would bring them out of the depths of the sea. After all, the very "winds have gone forth out of [His] mouth" (Ether 2:24).

Deliverance, however, would not be automatic. The Lord made it clear to the brother of Jared that his party would not be able to survive their journey across the expansive oceans unless the Lord prepared them against the wind and the waves. Thus, when the Jaredites finally "set forth into the sea, commending themselves unto the Lord their God" (Ether 6:4), they did so with the confidence that they had been prepared and outfitted for the voyage by the Lord Himself. Their barges were built by divine design in a peculiar manner—"tight like unto a dish" (Ether 2:17)—with a unique ventilation scheme and a miraculous lighting system. Having been prepared by the Lord for the turbulence of the seas, the Jaredites, as foretold, "were many times buried in the depths of the sea, because of the mountain waves which broke upon them, and also the great and terrible tempests which were caused by the fierceness of the wind." Because they had precisely followed the Lord's instructions in preparing for their voyage, "when they were buried in the deep there was no water that could hurt them, their vessels being tight like unto a dish" (Ether 6:7).

Many might have foolishly prayed for the winds to cease so that they could have had smoother sailing. By contrast, the Jaredites probably realized that, as Elder John Groberg has pointed out, "An experienced sailor does not fear storms or heavy seas, for they contain the lifeblood of sailing—wind. What experienced sailors fear is no wind, or being becalmed!"[1] Though the wind might create terrifyingly tall waves, the lack of wind creates another truly mortifying danger: stagnancy. Without wind, there would have been no progress toward land, resulting eventually in a slow and painful death, stranded at sea.

Thus, the record reflects that the Jaredites rejoiced despite—or perhaps even because of—the raging winds:

> And it came to pass that the wind did never cease to blow towards the promised land while they were upon the waters; and thus they were driven forth before the wind.
>
> And they did sing praises unto the Lord; yea, the brother of Jared did sing praises unto the Lord, and he did thank and praise the Lord all the day long; and when the night came, they did not cease to praise the Lord (Ether 6:8–9).

More shortsighted travelers might have resented the winds that made for remarkably rough sailing, but the Jaredites seem to have understood that such winds were propelling them to their destination.

SAILING OR SINKING

Wind is not invariably the sailor's friend. Without proper training, skill, and equipment, the same winds that help some sail can sink others. The Lord underscored this fact to the brother of Jared. He explained the conditions he would encounter would be so challenging that "ye cannot cross this great deep *save I prepare you* against the waves of the sea, and the winds which have gone forth, and the floods which shall come" (Ether 2:25; emphasis added).

Similarly, affliction does not guarantee sanctification. As Anne Morrow Lindbergh has observed, "If suffering alone taught, all the world would be wise, since everyone suffers."[2] In fact, the same trials and tribulations that draw some closer to the Lord can drive others away from the Lord. In a poignant aside near the end of the Book of Alma, Mormon notes one example of the double-edged sword of adversity:

But behold, because of the exceedingly great length of the war between the Nephites and the Lamanites *many had become hardened,* because of the exceedingly great length of the war; *and many were softened* because of their afflictions, insomuch that they did humble themselves before God, even in the depth of humility (Alma 62:41; emphasis added).

In other words, as Elder Dallin H. Oaks notes, the issue is not whether we will have adversity in our lives but what role we will let adversity play: "Adversity will be a constant or occasional companion for each of us throughout our lives. We cannot avoid it. The only question is how we will react to it. Will our adversities be stumbling blocks or stepping-stones?"[3]

Illustration 1.1 graphically depicts this phenomenon. Afflictions inevitably fly through our lives like a wedge. Adversity lifts some of us closer to God, even as it pushes others down and drives them further from God.

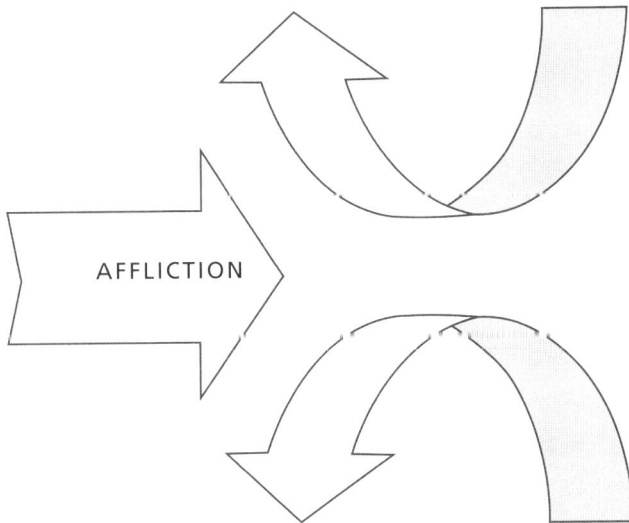

ILLUSTRATION 1.1: THE WEDGE OF AFFLICTION

Asking for help. What enables people to remain in positive territory so that their afflictions will help them become better rather than bitter toward God? Book of Mormon prophets give us several suggestions, perhaps none more direct than Jacob's: "Look unto God with firmness of mind, and pray unto him with exceeding faith, and he will console you in your afflictions, and he will plead your cause, and send down justice upon those who seek your destruction" (Jacob 3:1). Jacob's message is consistent with the Lord's object lesson centuries earlier to the Jaredites: without God's help, they could never hope to cross the great deep (Ether 2:25). Similarly, without divine assistance, we cannot withstand some of the mountain waves of affliction we will encounter in this life. Seeking God's aid in times of affliction is certainly one key to enduring well.

Enlightened expectations. A second key to avoiding bitterness is having realistic expectations about how the Lord is likely to help us. The Lord promised Jacob that He would eventually bring down justice upon his enemies. But the more immediate blessing was divine comfort rather than elimination of opposition—which is, after all, necessary in all things (see 2 Nephi 2:11). When we are drowning in a sea of afflictions, God is more likely to throw us a rope than to drain the sea. For example, when the people of Alma the Elder became subject to the vengeful Amulon, the Lord "did strengthen them that they could bear up their burdens with ease" (Mosiah 24:15). Eventually he lifted their heavy loads, but initially he simply strengthened their backs. Thus, the spiritually mature, like Alma, pray for strength to endure their trials: "O Lord, wilt thou grant unto me that I may have strength, that I may suffer with patience these afflictions which shall come upon me" (Alma 31:31). Those who expect more immediate relief may find themselves frustrated with and, eventually, embittered toward God.

In my own season of greatest trial and most effective prayer, I remember praying to Heavenly Father for a particular blessing. Like millions of people throughout the world, my mother was suffering the tragic effects of a disease similar to Alzheimer's, which robbed her mind of its usual powers of clear thinking. Kneeling in prayer, I pled with the Lord not to remove the illness but to alter and mitigate the nature of the delusions from which she suffered. Almost immediately the answer came that I was praying for the wrong thing. I was given to know that the nature of her difficult delusions would not change and that I needed to pray instead for strength for her and our family to be able to cope with this particular trial.

Gratitude amidst affliction. Third, remaining grateful in spite of afflictions is a trademark of those who are lifted up rather than weighed down by their trials. Nephi, in particular, exhibited this attribute with remarkable resolution.[4] He began his record by declaring that he had "seen many afflictions in the course of [his] days," but was then quick to add, "nevertheless, having been highly favored of the Lord in all my days . . ." (1 Nephi 1:1). Similarly, when his family's party arrived at Bountiful, Nephi noted that "notwithstanding we had suffered many afflictions and much difficulty, yea, even so much that we cannot write them all, we were exceedingly rejoiced when we came to the seashore" (1 Nephi 17:6). When Nephi was bound by his brothers so tightly that he "could not move" (1 Nephi 18:12) for four tempestuous days of life-threatening sailing, with his wrists and ankles painfully swollen (see 1 Nephi 18:15), he described his attitude: "Nevertheless, I did look unto my God, and I did praise him all the day long; and I did not murmur against the Lord because of mine afflictions" (1 Nephi 18:16). Years later, after some of his most difficult trials, Nephi wrote, "My God hath been my support; he hath led me through mine afflictions in the wilderness; and he hath preserved me upon the waters of the great deep" (2 Nephi 4:20). Acknowledging the Lord and His blessings in his life—even in the midst of affliction—may well have helped make it possible for Nephi's afflictions, like his brother Jacob's, to be consecrated for his gain (see 2 Nephi 2:2). Indeed, according to Elder Dallin H. Oaks, the scriptures "show that we should even give thanks for our afflictions because they turn our hearts to God and give us opportunities to prepare for what God would have us become."[5]

The virtue of patience. Finally, perhaps no virtue is more important in coping gracefully with affliction than patience—a virtue that is woven throughout the story of Ammon and his brethren. During their unique missionary training in the wilderness, the Lord cautioned Ammon and his party about the troubles they would encounter and how to deal with them: "Ye shall be patient in long-suffering and afflictions, that ye may show forth good examples unto them in me" (Alma 17:11). Later, Alma's heart was full of sorrow when he discovered his brethren had been imprisoned, bound with strong cords, and deprived of their clothes, food, and drink. In the midst of these afflictions they had been true to the counsel they had received from the Lord and had been "patient in all their sufferings" (Alma 20:29). In his joyful summation of their missionary endeavors, Ammon reported, "we have been patient in our sufferings, and we have suffered every privation" (Alma 26:28). However, they did not arrive at such patience without some divine prodding and reassurance: "Now when our hearts were depressed, and we were about to turn back, behold, the Lord comforted us, and said: Go amongst thy brethren, the Lamanites, and bear with patience thine afflictions, and I will give unto you success" (Alma 26:27).

In some situations, as with the people of Alma the Elder, the very purpose of tribulation may be to try our patience: "Nevertheless the

Lord seeth fit to chasten his people; yea, he trieth their patience and their faith" (Mosiah 23:21). Alma's people passed their test with flying colors. "[T]hey did submit cheerfully and with patience to all the will of the Lord" (Mosiah 24:15). King Benjamin implied such submissiveness to the will of the Lord is at the very core of patience. To become saints through the Atonement of Christ, according to King Benjamin, one must learn to be "patient, full of love, willing to submit to all things which the Lord seeth fit to inflict upon him, even as a child doth submit to his father" (Mosiah 3:19). In sum, the Book of Mormon is replete with admonitions to be patient in affliction[6] and commendations for those who are.[7]

Mourning without murmuring. This does not mean the Lord expects us to happily shrug off all afflictions with a knowing smile. During Laman and Lemuel's mutiny on the voyage to the promised land, Nephi notes that young Jacob and Joseph "were grieved because of the afflictions of their mother" (1 Nephi 18:19). Nephi considered his own "afflictions were great above all" and admitted he was "overcome because of [his] afflictions" (1 Nephi 15:5). And Jacob sounded downright glum in concluding his record, describing his family as "a lonesome and a solemn people, wanderers, cast out from Jerusalem, born in tribulation, in a wilderness, and hated of our brethren," and who "did mourn out our days" (Jacob 7:26).

The key is not to let such mourning slip into murmuring, as the daughters of Ishmael did after the death of their father (see 1 Nephi 16:35). Similarly, when Nephi's bow snapped, so did much of his family's resolve. "[B]ecause of their sufferings and afflictions in the wilderness[,]" Laman, Lemuel, the sons of Ishmael, and even Lehi began to "murmur against the Lord" (1 Nephi 16:20). Thus, the same afflictions that were consecrated to the gain of Jacob (see 2 Nephi 2:2) hardened the hearts of some of his older brothers—and, temporarily, even his prophet father. Yet even if we do cross the line from under-standable frustration with our trials to unacceptable murmuring against the Lord, Lehi's example shows us we can repent from such hard-heartedness and still enjoy sweet redemption (see 1 Nephi 16:25; 2 Nephi 1:15).

THEREFORE, WHAT?

Before leaving on a family vacation one year, I set a goal to be more patient, especially with my children. Things actually went fairly well until a couple of days into the vacation, when my three-year-old son sheepishly informed me that he'd locked my keys in the minivan. Unfortunately, my wife's keys were also in the minivan. Visions of vainly struggling to break in to our van filled my head, followed by the expense of hiring a locksmith. Soon I could sense the frustration and irritability bubbling up within me and approaching the spillover point. But in a rare moment of spiritual restraint, I decided to pray for help. I wasn't quite bright enough to pray for help to fight my impatience; instead, I asked for a way to get the keys back. But that was close enough for our merciful Heavenly Father, who sent me this simple thought: *It's a test.*

My patience goal for the trip immediately came to mind, along with the realization that I really hadn't been tested yet. Suddenly, I saw things in an entirely different light. It was as if I'd thought I'd been playing a game whose point was to get the keys back, but the Lord taught me that the actual objective of the game was to remain patient, no matter how long it took or how much it cost to get the keys. "It's okay," I assured my baffled son as I got up from my knees. "We'll get the keys back somehow. Thanks for telling me."

Locking keys in the car while away from home pales in compari-son to the afflictions that try our souls most. Still, the insight from that simple test has helped me finally come around in much more severe trials. After wondering what my mother was supposed to be getting out of years of dying slowly and losing her mental faculties, it finally occurred to me that she probably wasn't being tested any longer. My guess was that she'd already passed her test in life with flying colors. But those of us who loved her and who needed to serve her in these difficult circumstances were still being tested, and I, for one, wasn't doing too well on the test. When I stopped asking, "Why this disease? Why my mother?" and started asking, "What wouldst thou have me learn from this experience?" I began to feel refined rather than burned by the trying situation.

Such soul-stretching opportunities are inevitable for disciples of Christ, although they sometimes come when we'd rather relax or rest on our laurels for a bit. After so much traveling just to reach the shores of the great ocean, for example, the Jaredites must have been tempted to make their permanent home on some beachfront property, without making the final voyage across the great deep.[8] The Lord, however, had greater things in store for them: "And the Lord would not suffer that they should stop beyond the sea in the wilderness, but he would that they should come forth even unto the land of promise, which was choice above all other lands, which the Lord God had preserved for a righteous people" (Ether 2:7). Similarly, the Lord sees greater things in store for us—promised places preserved for righteous people—than we sometimes see for ourselves.

Yet He knows the journey to such sanctified sites requires a refining process fueled by affliction. Ultimately, He will tell those who are chosen, "I have refined thee, I have chosen thee in the furnace of affliction" (1 Nephi 20:10). Because He knows learning to endure adversity is a crucial part of the sanctification process, He may sometimes guide us through—rather than around—life's storms. That's why we can expect a journey fraught with what Elder Neal A. Maxwell calls "redemptive turbulence."[9] But because He loves us, He will always prepare us against the mountain waves and raging winds we will encounter, giving us an ability beyond our own to withstand them.

When we follow the instructions the Lord gives us to prepare for life's storms, we can pray with confidence when the storm rages. Yet despite our best efforts to button down the hatches in advance, we will still need God's help during the storm itself if we are to survive. If we feel compelled to hunker down and endure life's afflictions all on our own, we're bound to end up embittered rather than refined by the fire of tribulation.

On the other hand, our trials will sanctify us if we can somehow remain patient, trusting not only in the power but also in the timing of a loving Heavenly Father.[10] Although they may grouse from time to time about its ferocity, softened saints will ultimately thank God for the wind of affliction that goes forth out of His mouth because they recognize such wind propels them to their personal lands of promise.

OUR LIGHT IN THE WILDERNESS

*The Lord will light our way in the wilderness, just as he
lit the way for Lehi and others.*

When I was a brand new missionary in Goettingen, Germany, my companion and I were teaching an elderly gentleman who was kind but who was struggling to accept the gospel. In fact, with hindsight, I realize there's a fair chance he had Alzheimer's. In any event, my wise senior companion used an analogy in an attempt to teach this good brother the importance of being specific as he prayed to know if the Church was true. "If you had a feast laid out before you, and you wanted someone to give you the salt and pepper, you wouldn't ask him to pass you the food, would you? Instead, you'd be specific: you'd ask him to pass you the salt and pepper. It's the same way when we pray to Heavenly Father. If you want Him to tell you whether the Church is true, don't just pray for truth. Ask Him directly if the Church is true."

The elderly German nodded in agreement, so my companion asked him if he would offer such a prayer right then, together with us. The old man agreed, bowed his head, and began earnestly, "Heavenly Father, please pass the salt and pepper. . . ."

For a teacher, few things are more frustrating than when students remember an elaborate object lesson or analogy but not its point. Yet with many of us, that is just what seems to have happened with an incredible object lesson the Lord gave Lehi and his family in the wilderness en route to the promised land: we remember the Lord did not allow Lehi's family to use fire on their journey, but we often forget what the Lord hoped would be learned from this remarkable exercise. When we understand the reason behind God's burn ban, we can see how the experience of Lehi's family is part of an exodus pattern rich with symbolism[1] for our own journeys through life's wildernesses.

THE OBJECT LESSON

After traveling in the wilderness for eight years, Lehi's family finally arrived at a seaside location rich with fruit—a place so lush they called it Bountiful. There the Lord commanded Nephi to build a ship, which he did using tools constructed with the help of fire and bellows. This mention of fire prompted Nephi to explain that as his family made their journey in the wilderness, "the Lord had not hitherto suffered that we should make much fire." Instead, the Lord made their food sweet so that they did not need to cook it. He also lit the way on their journey (1 Nephi 17:4–13).

If the Lord's object lesson for Lehi's family was miraculously sweetening the meat and lighting the way without fire, what was the point of the object lesson? Hugh Nibley noted that the Lord's burn ban for Lehi's fleeing family was consistent with practice of even modern travelers in this region, who feared open fires would "attract the attention of a prowling raiding party over long distances and invite a night attack."[2] Other scholars have echoed this strain.[3] As one author notes, "Commentators have usually explained that this [limitation on using fire] was to avoid contact with unfriendly groups."[4] When I ask students why the Lord did not allow Lehi's family to use much fire, if students have an answer, they almost always answer along these same lines.

God's command to Lehi's family may well have been prompted by such practical considerations.[5] Yet if Nephi was aware of such a motivation for God's disallowance of fire, he chose not to mention it in his record.[6] Instead, Nephi offered the Lord's own explanation:

> I will also be your light in the wilderness; and I will prepare the way before you, . . . and ye shall know that it is by me that ye are led.
>
> . . . After ye have arrived in the promised land, ye shall know that I, the Lord, am God; and that I, the Lord, did deliver you from destruction; yea, that I did bring you out of the land of Jerusalem (1 Nephi 17:13–14).

Whether or not these miracles were prompted by security concerns, the Lord clearly wanted Lehi's family to learn a spiritual lesson from them: without the miraculous intervention of the Lord's nurturing and guiding hand, they would have been destroyed in a city of sin rather than being led to a land of promise. They would be delivered by *the Lord*, not merely by their own cleverness or hard work.

THE PATTERN

We've already made mention of the Jaredites, who over a thousand years earlier than Lehi's people made a similarly miraculous journey to the land of promise. Faced with the specter of being tossed on the waves for months on end in complete darkness, the brother of Jared pleadingly called the lack of light to the Lord's attention. In response, the Lord acknowledged that the usual methods, such as windows and fire, obviously would not do under the circumstances (see Ether 2:19–23). He then pointed the brother of Jared not to the specific solution to his light problem, but to the ultimate Source: "[W]hat will ye *that I should prepare* for you that ye may have light when ye are swallowed up in the depths of the sea?" (Ether 2:25; emphasis added).

In a temporal application of Nephi's teaching that we are saved by grace after all we can do (see 2 Nephi 25:23), the brother of Jared then did all that he could—forging sixteen small, transparent stones out of rock—and humbly laid his project before the Lord to be miraculously finished (see Ether 3:1–4) by the Finisher of our faith (see Moroni 6:4). Because of the brother of Jared's faith, the Lord blessed this prophet's plan and "caused stones to shine in darkness, to give light unto men, women, and children, that they might not cross the great waters in darkness" (Ether 6:3). So accompanied on their journey by "light continually," the Jaredites arrived nearly a year later "upon the shore of the promised land" (Ether 6:10–12).

The experience of Lehi's family, then, fits neatly into this scriptural pattern: God lights the way for his chosen people to lead them to their promised lands. He leads them out of captivity (Egypt),[7] confusion (Babel),[8] and destruction (Jerusalem) through dangerous wildernesses and sometimes over, or even through, tumultuous seas to far away lands of plenty. He does so in miraculous ways that make His delivering role unmistakably clear. In each case, a new nation is born with a divine birthmark to be remembered for generations to come.

THEREFORE, WHAT?

When I saw some success in learning German as a young missionary—like many other missionaries—I was occasionally complimented on how quickly I had picked up the language. Foolishly, when receiving such praise, my initial reaction was to explain that we had worked hard in the Missionary Training Center and that we diligently studied the language every morning. Eventually, the Spirit penetrated my pride and reminded me of the obvious: the only reason I could speak German as well as I did was that the Lord had enabled me to do so as one of His missionaries. In fact, I came to realize that such situations were great opportunities to help others see the hand of the Lord in the work we were doing.

For me, the challenge is to recognize God's hand in my life not only when he intervenes dramatically, but also when He subtly guides me. How often do I desperately plead for the Lord's help before a talk or test or interview, only to find myself forgetting the Lord afterwards and wondering what I'd gotten so worked up about? Given our natural tendency to claim sole credit for our successes, the Lord sometimes blesses us in unmistakable ways so that we will not miss what should be obvious: we have been led, nourished, and protected by Him in all our successful journeys.

This was true for Lehi and his family temporally, and it is true for all of us spiritually. Jacob taught that Christ is typified by "all things which have been given of God from the beginning of the world" (2 Nephi 11:4).[9] So it's not surprising that the greatest symbolism and lessons to be drawn from Lehi's fire-free years center on Christ, whose light enables all men and women to escape confusion and distinguish between good and evil while choosing for themselves which way to walk.[10] And unlike fires and flashlights and other man-made sources of light, His flame is inextinguishable to His followers: "I will be a light unto them forever, that hear my words" (2 Nephi 10:14) and will "disperse the powers of darkness from before" us (D&C 21:6). As Isaiah taught metaphorically, those who fear the Lord and obey his voice will always have light, but those who "compass [themselves] about with sparks" of their own intellectual creation and "walk in the light of [their] fire" (2 Nephi 7:11) will be sorely disappointed in the end.

Above all, through his atoning sacrifice, Jesus Christ makes possible our redemption from a world of sin, carrying us "beyond this vale of sorrow into a far better land of promise" (Alma 37:45). Just as Lehi's family undoubtedly knew when they arrived in their land of promise that it was by Him they were led (see 1 Nephi 17:13), their account reminds me that I must do more to remember that it is Christ who "did deliver [me] from destruction; yea, that [he] did bring [me] out of" lands of spiritual captivity, confusion, and destruction (see 1 Nephi 17:14).

WHEN FLEEING IS HONORABLE

If we are to remain separate from the wicked, we're often the ones who must do the moving.

For six months as a teenager I was blessed to live in the heart of Washington, D.C. One afternoon I decided to go running alone from the Capitol to the Washington Monument. About halfway through my jog, I noticed a group of local kids had started to run behind me. They looked to be about three or four years younger than I was, but there were several of them and one of me. They called to me, but I ignored them and looked straight ahead as I ran. Then their leader ran alongside me, told me not to ignore him when he talked to me, and suddenly hit me in the jaw with a right hook. Stunned but infused with adrenaline, I instinctively sprinted as fast as I could until I was able to find the safety of a police officer outside one of the museums lining the Mall.

Back at my apartment, I nursed my aching jaw and wondered whether I should have somehow stood my ground. Later, a friend pointed out the obvious: outnumbered as I was, running was a much smarter thing to do than fighting.

Fleeing is not the kind of military maneuver or social tactic we tend to glorify. Medals are awarded to people who lead charges, not retreats. The heroes of modern film and literature are usually those who stand their ground, not those who back down. And in many circumstances, leading a charge or standing our ground is exactly what the Lord would have us do.

Yet, occasionally, fleeing from overwhelming wickedness is the only way we can remain true to our standards. The experience of Book of Mormon civilization is not so different from our day: when it becomes necessary for the righteous to be separated from the wicked, it's usually the righteous who must do the moving. They do so as a last resort, often after first trying to save those from whom they eventually flee. But when wickedness reaches a boiling point, God's people are often forced to choose whether to stay where they are—and remain in the midst of sin, or run away—and remain in the grace of God. Through their example, Book of Mormon prophets and their followers teach us that fleeing can sometimes be the most courageous thing we can do.

PHYSICALLY FLEEING

We read no more than one chapter and a verse into the Book of Mormon before the first prophet is commanded to "take his family and depart into the wilderness" (1 Nephi 2:2). Although this involved leaving behind many material possessions and maybe even siblings, parents, and extended family, Lehi's choice was simple: flee or perish. "Wherefore, if my father should dwell in the land after he hath been commanded to flee out of the land, behold, he would also perish. Wherefore," wrote Nephi, with typical understatement, "it must needs be that he flee out of the land" (1 Nephi 3:18).

After Lehi's death, Nephi was commanded to "depart from [Laman and Lemuel] and flee into the wilderness," along with "all those who would go with" him. He obeyed, as did Zoram, Sam, Jacob, Joseph, and Nephi's sisters, who accepted his invitation to accompany him. Those who responded were "those who believed in the warnings and the revelations of God" (2 Nephi 5:5–6).

Centuries later, this scenario virtually repeated itself when the Lord commanded King Mosiah I "that he should flee out of the land of Nephi, and as many as would hearken unto the voice of the Lord should also depart out of the land with him, into the wilderness." Again, the exodus included any believers who would heed God's warning: "And they departed out of the land into the wilderness, as many as would hearken unto the voice of the Lord" (Omni 1:12–13).

Although Abinadi stayed to the fiery end of his ministry, his only convert (of whom we are aware) was called to take a different course, fleeing from his former employer and writing the words of Abinadi while in hiding (see Mosiah 17:4). Alma the Elder preached secretly near the waters of Mormon, but word soon leaked out to King Noah, who sent troops to destroy the budding religious movement. Forewarned by the Lord, Alma and his people "fled eight days' journey into the wilderness" and arrived at "a very beautiful and pleasant land, a land of pure water" (Mosiah 23:1–4).

In a final example of flight to escape unrighteousness, after many of their brethren were slaughtered by unconverted Lamanites the people of Anti-Nephi-Lehi prayed (at Ammon's prodding) about whether to leave their homeland and go to live among the Nephites. The Lord's answer, delivered through Ammon, was unequivocal: "Get this people out of this land, that they perish not; for Satan has great hold on the hearts of the Amalekites, who do stir up the Lamanites to anger against their brethren to slay them" (Alma 27:12).

In each of these cases of physical flight, the pattern is the same: the overall wickedness of a group of people becomes so great that it threatens the safety of the righteous who live among them. The Lord then warns those who wish to follow Him to flee, and they are faced with the choice to flee the wicked or perish.[1] God's invitation extends to everyone: all who are willing to follow His prophets are invited to flee wickedness to find safety.

SPIRITUAL FLIGHTS

Each act of flight described so far was physical; innocent people were instructed to flee violent enemies for their own safety. Yet these experiences illustrate an important spiritual point made by Alma the Younger: "And now I say unto you, all you that are desirous to follow the voice of the good shepherd, *come ye out from the wicked, and be ye separate, and touch not their unclean things*" (Alma 5:57; emphasis added). If we truly wish to follow the Savior, Alma teaches, we cannot afford to have a summer home in Babylon. Indeed, to become one with the Savior we must break up with the world; thus, sanctification often requires separation (see Leviticus 20:24, 26). Furthermore, this separation will not occur by encouraging the wicked to go away from the righteous; instead, it is the righteous who must "come . . . out from the wicked" (Alma 5:57).

THEREFORE, WHAT?

As we strive to be the leaven of righteousness in an increasingly unrighteous world, we continually face challenges in deciding how to lift others up without being dragged down. The Lord's counsel through Alma still applies with equal force to us: "Come ye out from the wicked, and be ye separate, and touch not their unclean things" (Alma 5:57). Yet, as in Alma's day, we live in pluralistic societies—with people living side by side who hold all sorts of different religious beliefs (or no religious beliefs at all). Thus, the ways in which we must remain separate from the wicked are now more subtle and complicated than simply pulling up roots and relocating our families.

Instead, the Lord's warnings to flee will more likely apply to decisions about our friendships, our activities, and our entertainment than to the location of our homes.

Reaching out. Knowing when to flee and when to stay is not a simple matter. If we were to hang out only with those who are perfect, even our Church buildings would go completely unused. Most members of today's worldwide Church inevitably work, attend school, and associate with those who do not share our beliefs or our commitment to gospel principles. President Gordon B. Hinckley has reminded us repeatedly to "be a little more tolerant and friendly to those not of our faith, going out of our way to show our respect for them. We cannot afford to be arrogant or self-righteous. It is our obligation to reach out in helpfulness, not only to our own but to all others as well."[2] Indeed, how can Daniel's vision of the kingdom of God rolling forth to fill the earth (Daniel 2:44–45) be fulfilled if we remain geographically isolated in insulated pockets of righteousness?[3] Speaking of our humanitarian efforts, Elder Glenn L. Pace made a statement equally applicable to our evangelical efforts: "We cannot become the salt of the earth if we stay in one lump in the cultural halls of our beautiful meetinghouses."[4]

Striking the balance. How, then, do we balance the need to lift and provide leaven to the world with the commandment to come out from the wicked and their unclean things? For starters, we can flee from certain activities—such as drinks after work or going to inappropriate entertainment with colleagues or friends—without withdrawing our association altogether. If we are clear about our standards, many of our friends and colleagues will respect our choice to hold to those standards, even if they do not adopt them themselves. We can often work well together on weekdays with those whose weekend and even weeknight lifestyle choices differ significantly from ours.

When I lived in Seattle, I would regularly associate with a friend from work who was an agnostic Jew. We talked freely and openly about our personal lives, including my Church callings. When he asked on more than one occasion whether I'd seen a critically acclaimed R-rated film, I finally told him that I didn't see such films until I could see an edited version. As diplomatically as I could, I also explained why I had adopted that policy. He understood completely and never belittled my decision or attempted to sway me from it. For me, how my friends (whether LDS or not) react to my standards is a great litmus test for whether I feel comfortable spending time with them. *Agreeing* with my standards has not been a prerequisite to friendship, but *respecting* them has.

The tipping point. Yet there are clearly situations and seasons when piecemeal withdrawal is not enough. In emphasizing the importance of mingling with our neighbors, Elder M. Russell Ballard was careful to note that he was not "suggesting that we should associate in any relationship that would place us or our families at spiritual risk."[5] The Savior speaks graphically to circumstances where sin and temptation reach a tipping point that requires us to sever friendships and ties altogether: "And if thy right hand offend thee, cut it off, and cast it from thee: for it is profitable for thee that one of thy members should perish, and not that thy whole body should be cast into hell" (Matthew 5:30). When friends or colleagues choose not to respect our decision to hold to different standards, their influence on us may become so damaging that we must cut off our relationships with them or risk getting spiritual gangrene.

The same analysis can be applied to activities and entertainment. The consumption of alcohol, for example, is part of many company-sponsored social events, such as Christmas parties. We may well choose to attend such events, obviously without drinking alcohol ourselves. But if the general tenor and spirit of an activity becomes simply incompatible with the Spirit, we may find the time has come where refraining from drinking is not enough: we must refrain from attending at all if we hope to have the Spirit with us. Moreover, our exit may be necessary so that we are not "tempted above that which [we] can bear" (Alma 13:28).

In our entertainment choices we may initially be able to combat unacceptable levels of profanity, nudity, or violence in films and television by taking advantage of technological screening devices and edited videos or waiting until movies are shown on television. But as the amount of unacceptable content in such entertainment increases, we may reach the point where we must flee altogether from watching certain shows. Similarly, if we or our children struggle with viewing pornography on the Internet, we may initially be able to combat such problems by implementing filters, placing computers only in common areas, or using other safeguards. But if problems persist, we may have to choose between giving up Internet access and giving up spiritual access.

Making the decision. In sum, sometimes we should fight to maintain our standards while living among or associating with those who live differently. But in specific aspects of our lives, such as friendships and entertainment choices, staying where we are may expose us to too much spiritual risk. Whether we have reached a point where we should flee from wickedness altogether should be a matter of personal prayer. The Nephites prayed over similar dilemmas in military matters: "And this was their faith, that by so doing God would . . . *warn them to flee, or to prepare for war,* according to their danger" (Alma 48:15; emphasis added). Because God knows our circumstances and our hearts intimately, when we turn to Him for guidance, we can trust that He will warn us to flee if the danger becomes too great for us to bear.[6] As we seek guidance in such matters in our day, a simple rule of thumb may be useful: when in doubt, get out.

Like the Nephites, I need to be willing to seek the Lord's guidance in determining whether to stay or flee in certain situations. Too often I'm afraid to ask for God's input because I fear the answer may cause me to give up something on which I've set my heart. Yet a willingness to act on the answer is usually a prerequisite to getting one. King Anti-Nephi-Lehi demonstrated such submissiveness when his people were deciding whether to stand their ground among the Lamanites or flee to join the Nephites, as Ammon had suggested. "Inquire of the Lord, and if he saith unto us go, we will go; otherwise we will perish in the land" (Alma 27:10). The Lord's response to Ammon was unequivocal: "Get this people out of this land, that they perish not; for Satan has great hold on the hearts of the Amalekites, who do stir up the Lamanites to anger against their brethren to slay them" (Alma 27:12).

As the influence of the adversary in a given environment increases, so does our danger. There is no question that we should always strive to change and improve our environments and combat Satan's influence. But as the experience of Book of Mormon people demonstrates, sometimes Satan's influence is simply too great. Then, if we are willing to seek and follow the Lord's counsel, He will warn us to flee, often inviting all who are willing to follow us as we depart. When He does, fleeing is truly an act of courage.

LESSONS ON
PERSPECTIVE

RECOGNIZING GOD'S HAND SO WE CAN HEAR HIS VOICE

As we ponder how merciful the Lord has been to us, our gratitude paves the way for revelation.

I once tried to help one of my young daughters master some of the fundamentals of softball. She bristled at my suggestions—noting she had already played T-ball for *two years,* thank you, so I decided there wasn't much point in trying to help her improve her game. Since she did not seem to appreciate the help I was giving her, I confess that I declined to offer further assistance.

My decision to stop helping her was probably impatient and unjustified, but my experience does underscore one of the critical ingredients in the revelatory process. Few scriptures summarize the potent formula for learning truth more succinctly and clearly than Moroni 10:4–5. Occasionally, our discussion of Moroni's promise also includes a cursory look at verse 3. From verse 3, we add the word *ponder* to the list of things we should do in order to receive a witness that the Book of Mormon is true. In our rush to verses 4 and 5, however, we sometimes overlook what Moroni is actually asking us to ponder. More fully appreciating the important principle Moroni teaches us in that verse can help us become more receptive not only to a confirmation of the Book of Mormon's truthfulness, but also to revelation in general.

THE PONDERING PREREQUISITE

At the conclusion of Moroni 10:3, Moroni charges readers who "receive these things" to "ponder it in your hearts." At first blush, we may think Moroni is asking us to ponder the principles we have read in the Book of Mormon. However, upon closer scrutiny, it becomes apparent that Moroni is asking us to ponder something much more precise:

> Behold, I would exhort you that when ye shall read these things . . . that ye would remember *how merciful the Lord hath been* unto the children of men, from the creation of Adam even down until the time that ye shall receive these things, and ponder it in your hearts (Moroni 10:3; emphasis added).

Pondering the teachings of the Book of Mormon in general is undoubtedly a worthwhile exercise. But when Moroni asks readers to "ponder it in your hearts," he is inviting us to ponder just how merciful the Lord has been to His children throughout the history of the world, right down to the time we mercifully receive the Book of Mormon.

Moroni echoes a theme first sounded by Nephi in the first chapter of the Book of Mormon. Nephi vowed to "show unto [his readers] that the tender mercies of the Lord are over all those whom he hath chosen" (1 Nephi 1:20).[1] Many other prophets similarly recognized the Lord's mercy toward them individually and their people collectively. For example, on his deathbed, Lehi reflected on "how merciful the Lord had been in warning us that we should flee out of the land of Jerusalem" (2 Nephi 1:3). Jacob acknowledged "how merciful our God is unto us," particularly in light of Israel's stiffneckedness (Jacob 6:4). Alma the Younger asked his people whether they had "sufficiently retained in remembrance [the Lord's] mercy and longsuffering towards" their fathers (Alma 5:6), thus reminding us that God puts up with a lot from His children.[2]

ACKNOWLEDGING THE LORD'S HAND

These prophetic reminders are necessary because, like ungrateful children who take their mother's constant service for granted, natural men and women tend to overlook the ways in which God blesses them. We are sometimes among those whom Elder Neal A. Maxwell has said "boast of their independence from God" and thus "are like the goldfish in a bowl who regards himself as self-sufficient."[3] Such ingratitude ranks high on the list of sins that kindle God's wrath. Indeed, God singles out this sin for special mention: "And in nothing doth man offend God, or against none is his wrath kindled, save those who confess not his hand in all things, and obey not his commandments" (D&C 59:21).

While ingratitude in general kindles the Lord's wrath, failure to grasp the mercy proffered to us by the Atonement is particularly disappointing to the Lord. Thus, Zenock prayed, "Thou art angry, O Lord, with this people, because they will not understand thy mercies which thou hast bestowed upon them because of thy Son" (Alma 33:16). Whether we underestimate our need for the Atonement or His willingness to forgive us when we repent, our Heavenly Father despairs when His people sometimes just don't get the Atonement. Whether we deny the need for the Atonement altogether, overlook our need for it individually, or underestimate the breadth and depth of its reach, our failure to recognize that God has "turned away [His] judgments because of [His] Son" (Alma 33:13) is highly offensive to the Lord. In elaborating on what it means for God to be a jealous God, Elder Melvin J. Ballard spoke eloquently of the Father's agony in allowing His Son to suffer for our sins, concluding that the Father is "jealous lest we should [ever] ignore and forget and slight his greatest gift unto us."[4] As we contemplate how merciful the Lord has been to us, remembering the atoning sacrifice of Jesus Christ is surely at the heart of what Moroni asks us to ponder.

THE NEXUS BETWEEN PONDERING AND REVELATION

Our failure to recognize God's hand in our lives not only offends God, but also makes us less open to inspiration from Him. When we fail to see how He has blessed us already, we may lack the gratitude we need to plead successfully for additional heavenly guidance. In short, ungrateful hearts tend to be poor receptors of revelation. Conversely, gratitude paves the way for revelation.

The writer of Proverbs described the chemistry between gratitude and revelation in this way: "Trust in the Lord with all thine heart; and lean not unto thine own understanding. In all thy ways acknowledge him, and he shall direct thy paths" (Proverbs 3:5–6). In other words, *if* we acknowledge him, *then* he will direct our paths. As we realize how the Lord has blessed us, we become more willing to seek—and the Lord becomes more willing to grant—the direction we need to successfully navigate through the perils of this world. Whether we are praying to know the truthfulness of the Book of Mormon or of any other matter (see Moroni 10:5), our plea for divine direction will be most effective when we first recognize how indebted we are to God. Thus, if we find we are having difficulty hearing the Lord's voice in our lives, it may be because we are failing to recognize His hand in our blessings.

THEREFORE, WHAT?

A Church leader with whom I served for years and whom I deeply respect once explained how he gained a testimony during his teenage years, after drifting in and out of activity. A wise Sunday School teacher challenged him not just to pray for a testimony of the truth-fulness of the Book of Mormon and the Church, but first to take an important preparatory step: spend fifteen minutes doing nothing but thanking Heavenly Father for his blessings. The teacher's prescription for revelation was simple but effective. After fifteen minutes of pon-dering in prayer how merciful the Lord had been to him, my friend's heart was so swollen with gratitude that he quickly received an answer when he prayed about the truthfulness of the Book of Mormon and the Church.

If I am struggling to feel in tune with the Lord, I have often tried that same approach. Few things invite the Spirit more consistently and effectively for me than specifically acknowledging the Lord's hand in my life and thanking him for my blessings. Too often I find that I emu-late my daughter in her assumption that she needed no additional training in how to play softball, laughably thinking that I've got plenty of experience already and can figure things out on my own. When I manage to humble myself and acknowledge how richly I've been blessed and how desperately I still need more training from God, mercifully He directs my paths.

OF WHAT HAVE YE TO BOAST?

A false sense of spiritual self-sufficiency can blind us to God's mercy.

I once complimented a little girl at church on her lovely dress. "I bought it myself," replied the girl, with more than a twinge of satisfaction.

"Really? How did you get the money?" I asked, perhaps inappropriately.

"By doing chores," she answered without hesitation.

"What are your chores?" I pried.

"I make my bed *every* day," she boasted.

"And how much do you get paid for that?" I inquired, unquestionably venturing into inappropriately nosy territory. But she freely told me the amount, which was on the high end for allowances and was several times more than even an adult could have earned working as a maid making beds. Yet these facts were lost on my young friend, who seemed to believe that she was simply being paid the market rate for her wages. In her mind, she'd earned the money for the dress all on her own; there was no need to mention her parents, since they'd simply paid her what she was due.

Those of us who strive diligently to do our spiritual chores sometimes encounter a peculiar obstacle to remembering God's merciful hand in our lives. Because we recognize that we receive blessings only when we are obedient to the commandments on which those blessings are predicated (see D&C 130:20–21), we may slip into believing that our blessings are simply the natural consequence of our righteousness. "If we are not careful when everything is going just right in life," warned Elder Ben B. Banks, "there can be a temptation to forget our Heavenly Father and give credit to ourselves for our happy state."[1] If we do so, we foolishly buy into the mistaken viewpoint of Korihor, who taught that "every man fared in this life according to the management of the creature; therefore every man prospered according to his genius, and that every man conquered according to his strength" (Alma 30:17).

TURNING ON THE LIGHT

Understanding that righteousness triggers blessings is important because it can motivate us to be righteous. If there were no connection between our conduct and our blessings, finding the ongoing drive to be obedient would be more difficult. Connecting the little girl's performance of chores to the payment of the generous allowance was probably a wise parental move. But unfortunately, like the little girl, we sometimes assume that if some conduct on our part triggers a particular result, we can then claim complete credit for the result: If we are righteous, then we are blessed; therefore, we earn and fully deserve every blessing we get.

One way to discover the flaw in that conclusion is to consider the light in a classroom at church. If we flick on the light switch, then there is light. Knowing where the light switch is and how to turn it on are very valuable bits of enabling information. Yet to claim we alone are responsible for producing the light in the room would be absurd. Here's a quick list of others who deserve credit:

- The janitor who installed the light bulb;
- Thomas Edison and those who helped him invent the light bulb;
- The electricians who wired the room;
- The utility workers who laid the power lines to the Church;
- The workers who built and maintain the dam that generates the electricity that flows through the power lines;
- The Lord, who inspired Edison and provides the water for the dam and prospers His people so they are able to pay the tithing that pays the electric bill.

Without this infrastructure in place, we could flick the light switch all we wanted and nothing would happen. In much the same way, without an infrastructure of grace in place, our attempts to generate blessings for ourselves would be futile. The Book of Mormon helps us recognize this infrastructure of grace in our lives—the mercy inherent in each of the blessings we receive, even though those blessings may be triggered by righteousness. They teach that we are indebted to God because, among other reasons:

- He created us and lends us breath;
- He gives us commandments and the ability to recognize how we should live;
- He helps us repent and keep the commandments (particularly if we seek His aid);
- He gives us an incredible return on our investment of obedience; and, most significantly,
- Through the Atonement, He mercifully provides us with the ability to repent of our sins rather than fully suffer the consequences of our actions.

God created us. King Benjamin was clearly intent on helping his people understand their indebtedness to God. Perhaps like Moroni he understood that we are in the best position to receive revelation from God when we recognize how merciful He has been to us. Only after putting to rest any false conceptions of self-sufficiency would his people be prepared for the necessary mighty change of heart. King Benjamin bases his case for our indebtedness on two critical facts: God created us and He enables us to live from day to day.

> I say unto you, my brethren, that if you should render all the thanks and praise which your whole soul has power to possess, to that God who has created you, and has kept and preserved you, and . . . is preserving you from day to day, by lending you breath . . . I say, if ye should serve him with all your whole souls yet ye would be unprofitable servants. . . . [H]e hath created you, and granted unto you your lives, for which ye are indebted unto him (Mosiah 2:20–21, 23).

A mother deserves her child's eternal gratitude (whether or not she receives it) on the sole basis of the nausea, discomfort, trauma, risk, inconvenience, and sleep deprivation a mother endures to bring a child into the world. In much the same way, we are eternally indebted to our Heavenly Father—even if He blessed us in no other way—because He created us and preserves our lives from day to day. Yes, we may keep His commandments, King Benjamin acknowledges, but we make no inroads into paying down our debt through our obedience because the Lord "doth immediately bless [us]" (Mosiah 2:24). Hence, asks King Benjamin, "of what have ye to boast?" (Mosiah 2:24). King Benjamin wants none of his people to labor under the misconception that God has somehow shortchanged them or that they are *due* further payments from Him. Instead, they have all been taught and know that they "are eternally indebted to [their] heavenly Father, to render to him all that [they] have and are" (Mosiah 2:34).

God gives us commandments and the ability to recognize how we should live. It is true that we trigger blessings by our obedience to commandments, but even knowing about the commandments we need to keep is a result of God's mercy. For example, as the Word of Wisdom demonstrates, God's commandments often mercifully steer us clear of dangers of which we would otherwise be unaware. As Elder Dallin H. Oaks put it, "I am also grateful for the warnings of the scriptures and Church leaders on things to avoid. By following that counsel I have been able to avoid pitfalls that might otherwise have trapped and enslaved me."[2]

Similarly, as discussed earlier, on several occasions in the Book of Mormon God warns His people to flee from danger. Just as we are blessed for obeying commandments, Lehi and the others were blessed for heeding the Lord's warning. Yet in each case (especially Lehi's departure from Jerusalem), the commandment itself was an act of divine mercy, alerting God's followers to dangers that might otherwise have been underestimated or would have remained unknown.

In a day when so many people are abandoning what once seemed the most indisputable of God's commandments, we are reminded of God's wisdom and mercy in warning us to avoid conduct the world tells us is acceptable and even desirable. Whether the commandment is chastity, charity, or honesty, standards of conduct that feel like spiritual common sense to some are apparently not so intuitive to those "who live without God in the world" (Mosiah 27:31). Indeed, one reason God's commandments may seem so obviously wise to the Latter-day Saints is the guiding gifts He has given to us "by the power of the Holy Ghost, which is the gift of God unto all those who diligently seek him" (1 Nephi 10:17), and also by the light of Christ.

Together, these gifts allow us to recognize how we ought to live. Of the light of Christ Mormon taught, "the Spirit of Christ is *given* to every man, that he may know good from evil" (Moroni 7:16–17; emphasis added).

Thus, even when good fortune seems to flow naturally from our good conduct, we must ask whether we would have been wise enough to live so well if we didn't have the light of Christ, the gift and power of the Holy Ghost, or merciful warnings from God's prophets. When we see things in this light, we can better understand King Anti-Nephi-Lehi's exclamation: "And the great God has had mercy on us, and made these things known unto us that we might not perish . . . because he loveth our souls . . . ; therefore, in his mercy he doth visit us by his angels, that the plan of salvation might be made known unto us as well as unto future generations. Oh, how merciful is our God!" (Alma 24:14–15).

God helps us repent and keep the commandments (especially as we seek His aid). As a young missionary, I often used a bridge to demonstrate how the Atonement worked. I would explain that a wide chasm of sin separates us from God and that without a bridge spanning that chasm, we could never return to the presence of God. Through His atoning sacrifice, Jesus Christ built just such a bridge, making it possible for us to return to live with Heavenly Father. However, with that merciful bridge in place, it is up to us to cross the bridge. If we do not, I explained, we will remain separated from God.

Though this analogy still seems largely accurate to me, as a bishop I came to believe an important addition is necessary: The Lord has not only built the bridge, but if we seek His aid, He will also help us cross the bridge. Clearly, without the bridge none of us could return to God. But even with the bridge of the Atonement in place, perhaps none of us would have the power to cross the bridge strictly on our own.

Though the Atonement makes repentance possible, most of us seem to need help from the Lord to be able to fully repent and take advantage of the Savior's marvelous gift. The purpose of the Atonement is not just to provide vouchers for forgiveness once we've completed the repentance process; it creates a pool of mercy that we can and should use in the very process of repenting.

The teachings and experience of Book of Mormon prophets demonstrate the importance of seeking the Lord's help in resisting temptation and repenting from sin. For example, after bemoaning the "temptations and the sins which do so easily beset me," Nephi acknowledges: "My God hath been my support" (2 Nephi 4:18, 20). Further, he pleads with the Lord for power to resist temptation: "Wilt thou make me that I may shake at the appearance of sin?" (2 Nephi 4:31).

One day, after I had emphasized the importance of seeking this enabling power of the Atonement in our lives, one of my students stayed after class, troubled. "I'm struggling with this," she said, as nearly as I can recall. "It just doesn't seem right. It seems like the whole point of being here on earth is to be tested and that it's almost like trying to cheat on the test if we don't do it alone." I tried to help this student understand that perhaps a part of the test itself is seeing whether we eventually learn that we really can't pass the test alone— that only when we turn to God for help in keeping the commandments can we find the strength we need to overcome our natural tendency to sin.

Elder David A. Bednar spoke passionately about the mindset that leads many of us to believe we are somehow cheating if we don't do it all alone:

Most of us clearly understand that the atonement is for sinners. I am not so sure, however, that we know and understand that the atonement is also for saints—for good men and women who are obedient and worthy and conscientious and who are striving to become better and serve more faithfully. I frankly do not think many of us "get it" concerning this enabling and strengthening aspect of the atonement, and I wonder if we mistakenly believe we must make the journey from good to better and become a saint all by ourselves, through sheer grit, willpower, and discipline, and with our obviously limited capacities. . . . There is help from the Savior for the entire journey of life—from bad to good to better and to change our very nature.[3]

King Benjamin's people clearly did "get it." A temple-going sort of people even before his sermon (see Mosiah 2:1–3), they pled for the atoning blood of Christ to be applied to them. Their prayer was not only that they might "receive forgiveness of [their] sins," but that their "hearts [might] be purified" (Mosiah 4:2). The result of their pleas was both a remission of sins and a dramatic change in their attitude toward sin and in their ability to resist temptation. "[T]he Spirit of the Lord Omnipotent," declared the people, "has wrought a mighty change in us, or in our hearts, that we have no more disposition to do evil, but to do good continually" (Mosiah 5:2).

The LDS Bible Dictionary adds some useful insights to this principle. It defines grace, in part, as that which enables individuals, "through faith in the atonement of Jesus Christ and repentance of their sins, [to] receive strength and assistance *to do good works that they otherwise would not be able to maintain if left to their own means. This grace is an enabling power*" (emphasis added). Thus, when Nephi teaches that "it is by grace that we are saved, after all we can do" (2 Nephi 25:23), such grace may refer not only to giving us second chances when we fall off the strait and narrow path, but also to the Lord's willingness to hold our hand to help us as we return to the path and strive to stay on it. Mercifully, the Lord still blesses us richly for such divinely aided obedience, much like the parents who pay their child for doing chores they helped the child perform.

God gives us an incredible return on our investment of obedience. Like the child who performs her chores, it turns out that we are paid an inflated wage. Without a loving Heavenly Father, for example, we could zealously observe the Word of Wisdom and might reap the positive consequences of avoiding lung cancer or emphysema. But to whom could we submit our demands for "wisdom and great treasures of knowledge, even hidden treasures" (D&C 89:19)? Fulfillment of such promises is conditioned on our faith and obedience. But without the presence of a loving Creator, these blessings would not be the inevitable consequence of our conduct. Without God, we might find ourselves in the same situation as a young child without loving parents—doing chores and keeping commandments, expecting generous allowances and rich blessings, only to discover the relatively limited worth of our efforts in the absence of a merciful benefactor. As Elder Neal A. Maxwell has pointed out, "God is quick to give us large blessings for our small obedience! Geometrically, if little gears were to represent our obedience and large gears God's generous blessings for us all, as they do, we could grasp even further insights into God's character!"[4]

Through the Atonement, the Lord mercifully provides us with the ability to repent of our sins rather than fully suffer the consequences of our actions. Some time ago, our family studied the law of the harvest powerfully described by Alma (see Alma 41). We learned that in the next life our works will be restored to us, good for good and evil for evil, and that what we send out will return to us again (see Alma 41:3–4, 15). As we read the last verse of the chapter, my wife and

I were taken aback when our eight-year-old daughter suddenly burst into tears. Puzzled, we asked, "What's the matter?"

"It's no good," she cried. "I won't able to live with you and Heavenly Father. I make too many mistakes."

We were impressed by how deeply our daughter had taken to heart the law of the harvest. She was coming to understand that, alone, we would be, as Alma put it, "in the grasp of justice; yea, the justice of God, which consigned [mankind] forever to be cut off from his presence" (Alma 42:14). We held our daughter in our arms as we explained that in the next chapter of Alma, we would learn about how we could live together as a family and with Heavenly Father, even though we had all sinned.

Fortunately for my daughter and all of us, there is a major footnote to the law of the harvest: because of the Atonement, through repentance we have a chance to erase the black marks left by sin. As Alma explained to his son, "Mercy claimeth the penitent, and mercy cometh because of the atonement" (Alma 42:23). Without the Atonement, whatever blessings we might merit through our obedience would be offset by our sins, and the balance would not be favorable. President James E. Faust reminds us with personal poignancy that what we really want is something better than we deserve: "I am frank to admit that when I say my prayers, I do not ask for justice; I ask for mercy."[5]

The Atonement is so much more than just another bullet point under the heading of grace. Of all the aspects of God's mercy, none is greater than the opportunity to repent, made possible by the Atonement. When we repent, God does not require us to repay all our debts before blessing us for our obedience to those commandments we manage to keep. Repentance grants us a clean slate and allows us to reap the blessings of our obedience without reaping all the consequences of our sins. When we are blessed for commandments we keep, we are often like the golfer who makes a hole in one—but only after hitting several mulligans. We may be tempted to rush into the clubhouse to brag about our accomplishment, but we would do well to remember King Benjamin's rhetorical reminder: "Of what have ye to boast?" (Mosiah 2:24).

When we reflect on how it is that we are able to receive blessings, we become less inclined to focus on our merits or, in the words of Paul, to go "about to establish [our] own righteousness" (Romans 10:3)—and more inclined to focus on the merits of the Savior. After all, it is the Atonement that makes our repentance—and thus our blessings—possible. Like King Anti-Nephi-Lehi, we might be moved to declare, "And I also thank my God, yea, my great God, that he hath granted unto us that we might repent of these things, and also that he hath forgiven us of those our many sins . . . which we have committed, and taken away the guilt from our hearts, through the merits of his Son" (Alma 24:10).

A CLARIFYING CAUTION

Given the adversary's fondness for perverting the doctrine of grace that is at the very center of the gospel of Jesus Christ, a clarifying caution is in order. What a shame it is when some misunderstand the doctrine of grace and foolishly use it as a rationale for letting up in their efforts to keep God's commandments. While it's critical that we recognize the Lord's merciful hand in our lives, it is also possible to become so fixated on God's mercy that we fall into the modern theological trap of thinking we do not need to strive to obey God's commandments and repent of our sins.

When we truly understand how merciful the Lord has been to us, that understanding should actually bolster our resolve to keep His commandments, not undermine it. Much as children who finally realize how inflated the wage is their parents pay them for doing chores, when we ponder how richly God blesses us for a little obedience, we should be all the more motivated to do what He asks of us. More important, the more we recognize how merciful God is to us, the more gratitude and love we will have in our hearts for Him. Such intensified love of God provides the most powerful kind of motivation for keeping His commandments.

THEREFORE, WHAT?

I fear that had I died earlier in my life, I might have been foolishly tempted to knock on the door of the kingdom of God to ask for my mansion, thinking I had earned one all on my own. What I have learned over the years in studying the Book of Mormon is that God does not open the door to His kingdom to any who think they fully deserve an inheritance there all on their own. The door opens only when we can truly confess in our hearts that the ultimate reason we hope to get in is that we're with Jesus Christ, that we stake any claim to entrance on him—"relying wholly upon the merits of him who is mighty to save" (2 Nephi 31:19).

It seems unlikely that we can ever receive the greatest of all God's gifts, even eternal life (see D&C 14:7), without realizing it *is* a gift, not merely the natural consequence of our hard work. The Book of Mormon helps us understand that obedience to God's laws fulfills the conditions He has set to bestow marvelous gifts upon us. In the words of *True to the Faith,* "Although all such blessings come as results of [our] obedience, [we] could never receive them through [our] efforts alone. They are merciful gifts from a loving and compassionate Father."[6]

YOU CANNOT CARRY THEM
WITH YOU

Given the fleeting nature of earthly wealth, there's not much point in hoarding it or setting our hearts on it.

Poverty is not the point of the Lord's plan for us. To the contrary, one of the most frequently repeated promises in the Book of Mormon is that those who keep God's commandments will prosper. This promise was often (though not exclusively) fulfilled in very temporal ways in Mormon's record.

Yet the acquisition of such prosperity is fraught with spiritual risk. Consequently, Book of Mormon prophets consistently and convincingly warn against the dangers of temporal riches. Indeed, this book of scripture—written for our day—speaks with sobering clarity about the intoxicating allure of the "vain things of this world." In a modern world that countenances and even promotes the unabashed accumulation of such vain things, the Book of Mormon provides refreshing relief and perspective. It warns us unequivocally against spending our lives to earn wealth that may corrupt us and will ultimately slip through our fingers. "Seek not after riches nor the vain things of this world," wrote Alma, "for behold, you cannot carry them with you" (Alma 39:14).

POVERTY IS NOT THE POINT

Near the outset of the Book of Mormon, the Lord taught Nephi the key to prospering in the remarkable land that awaited his family: "And inasmuch as ye shall keep my commandments, ye shall prosper, and shall be led to a land of promise; yea, even a land which I have prepared for you; yea, a land which is choice above all other lands" (1 Nephi 2:20). The Lord extended this same conditional promise of prosperity to Nephi's seed (see 1 Nephi 4:14). In vision, Nephi also saw that righteous Gentiles would one day prosper in the same land (see 1 Nephi 13:15–19). Of course, the most important aspect of this promise was spiritual, as evidenced by the promise's flip side: "and inasmuch as ye will not keep my commandments ye shall be cut off from my presence" (2 Nephi 4:4). Thus, the greatest sense in which we can prosper is to live so that we will not be separated from God.

However, Book of Mormon prophets also clearly considered temporal blessings to be a fulfillment of the Lord's promise of prosperity. Consider the following examples:

- In noting that he and his followers "did prosper exceedingly," Nephi amplified his statement by adding, "for we did sow seed, and we did reap again in abundance. And we began to raise flocks, and herds, and animals of every kind" (2 Nephi 5:11).
- The people of Alma "began to prosper by degrees in the land, and began to raise grain more abundantly, and flocks, and herds, that they did not suffer with hunger," much as "the Lord did visit [the people of King Mosiah] and prosper them, and they became a large and wealthy people" (Mosiah 21:16; 27:7).
- Of the righteous members of the Church in Alma the Younger's day, Mormon wrote, "And now, *because of the steadiness of the church* they began to be exceedingly rich, having abundance of

all things whatsoever they stood in need—an abundance of flocks and herds, and fatlings of every kind, and also abundance of grain, and of gold, and of silver, and of precious things, and abundance of silk and fine-twined linen, and all manner of good homely cloth. . . . And thus they did prosper and become far more wealthy than those who did not belong to their church" (Alma 1:29, 31; emphasis added).

Mormon clearly saw such temporal success as a fulfillment of the Lord's promise to Nephi. After describing the "prosperous circumstances" of the Nephites—including the fact that they had become "exceedingly rich"—Mormon concludes that the Lord's promise of prosperity to Lehi had been "verified" (Alma 50:17–20; emphasis added).

These passages demonstrate that the Lord clearly has no objection to his people successfully providing for their temporal needs. To the contrary, Book of Mormon experience shows such prosperity sometimes (but not always)[1] results from obedience to God's commandments.

A WARNING FOR OUR DAY

Even though—or perhaps even because—righteousness can lead to material blessings, the Book of Mormon denounces with particular power the abuse of such earthly earnings. As the prophetic editors of the book, Mormon and Moroni enjoyed a historical perch that gave them unique insights into the pitfalls of prosperity. First, having condensed and compiled the thousand-year history of his fallen people, Mormon could see with painful clarity the distressingly predictable pattern of righteousness, prosperity, pride, and sin:

And thus we can behold how false, and also the unsteadiness of the hearts of the children of men; yea, we can see that the Lord in his great infinite goodness doth bless and prosper those who put their trust in him.

Yea, and we may see at the very time when he doth prosper his people, . . . yea, then is the time that they do harden their hearts, and do forget the Lord their God, and do trample under their feet the Holy One—yea, and this because of their ease, and their exceedingly great prosperity (Helaman 12:1–2; emphasis added).

In addition to this historical perspective, Moroni and Mormon were privileged to have a glimpse forward into what would come. Appropriately, we often refer to Moroni's prophetic witness that he saw our day, but we sometimes forget what he saw in our time:

Behold, I speak unto you as if ye were present, and yet ye are not. But behold, Jesus Christ hath shown you unto me, and I know your doing.

And I know that ye do walk in the pride of your hearts; and there are none save a few only who do not lift themselves up in the pride of their hearts, unto the wearing of very fine apparel. . . .

For behold, ye do love money, and your substance, and your fine apparel, and the adorning of your churches, more than ye love the poor and the needy, the sick and the afflicted. . . .

Why do ye adorn yourselves with that which hath no life, and yet suffer the hungry, and the needy, and the naked, and the sick and the afflicted to pass by you, and notice them not? (Mormon 8:35–39).

In short, when given a glimpse of our day, Moroni saw, among other things, proud, materialistic people, indulging their wants and neglecting the poor.

In light of Moroni's vision, President Ezra Taft Benson's reminder that the Book of Mormon was "written for our day" is especially relevant as we study the Book of Mormon's teachings about prosperity and its dangers. Referring to Mormon and Moroni, President Benson queried: "If they saw our day, and chose those things which would be of greatest worth to us, is not that how we should study the Book of Mormon? We should constantly ask ourselves, 'Why did the Lord inspire Mormon (or Moroni or Alma) to include that in his record? What lesson can I learn from that to help me live in this day and age?'"[2]

In that light, it's interesting to note just how frequently Book of Mormon prophets warn us about the dangers of materialism. For example, the phrase *vain things* is used eleven times in the Book of Mormon, always in the context of the fleeting things this world has to offer. By contrast, the phrase *vain thing* or *things* appears only four times in the Old Testament and just once in the New Testament. Of those five biblical usages, only one (1 Samuel 12:21) is in the context of materialism. Book of Mormon prophets also warn repeatedly against "setting our hearts" on earthly attainments rather than eternal blessings, while the Bible rarely uses this phrase in this way.[3]

This is not to suggest that the Bible is void of warnings against materialism. Few scriptural passages, if any, more poignantly decry the hollowness of hedonism than the Savior's admonitions in the Sermon on the Mount, for example. There the Savior tells us we must choose whether to serve God or mammon (see Matthew 6:24), and He implores us not to lay up treasures for ourselves upon the earth, "where moth and rust doth corrupt, and where thieves break through and steal" (Matthew 6:19). Similarly, the author of Proverbs warns us of the transitory nature of wealth with this vivid imagery: "Labour not to be rich: . . . for riches certainly make themselves wings; they fly away as an eagle toward heaven" (Proverbs 23:4–5). But is it just coincidental that the Book of Mormon, written with our day in mind, warns against the dangers of materialism so much more frequently than the Bible? Perhaps Mormon and Moroni knew that the pursuit of fleeting pleasures and honors would present an unprecedented problem in our day of unparalleled wealth and consequent ease. [4]

THE TROUBLE WITH MONEY

Most of the prophetic concerns about prosperity that permeate the Book of Mormon can be grouped into three main categories. First, material blessings often lead to pride, either as we view ourselves in our prosperity as better than others or as we boast in our self-sufficiency. Second, the dazzling things of this world tend to distract us from things eternal and prompt us to set our hearts upon temporary rewards and pleasures. Finally, even if the accumulation of wealth does not distract us or lift us up in our own eyes, Jacob and King Benjamin provide some pointed advice on what prosperous Saints ought to do with their riches.

Prosperity leads to pride. In the Book of Mormon (as well as in our day), prosperity often leads to a certain sense of superiority—satisfaction not only in having material things but in having more of them than others do. Jacob lamented the onset of this development among his people as they settled into their new land and began pursuing riches:

> And the hand of providence hath smiled upon you most pleasingly, that you have obtained many riches; and *because some of you have obtained more abundantly than that of your brethren ye are lifted up in the pride of your hearts,* and wear stiff necks and high heads because of the costliness of your apparel, and persecute your brethren because ye suppose that ye are better than they (Jacob 2:13; emphasis added).

In the Book of Mormon, such pride almost invariably followed prosperity (see 4 Nephi 1:23–24; D&C 38:39) and eventually unraveled the peace that had been ushered in by the resurrected Savior's visit to the Americas: "The people . . . began to be proud in their hearts, *because of their exceeding riches. . . .* And from this time the disciples began to sorrow for the sins of the world" (4 Nephi 1:43–44; emphasis added). This kind of prosperity-induced pride is what C. S. Lewis described when he said, "Pride gets no pleasure out of having something, only out of having more of it than the next man. . . . It is the comparison that makes you proud: the pleasure of being above the rest."[5]

Jacob pleaded with his people to "let not this pride of your hearts destroy your souls!" (Jacob 2:16). After inviting his brethren to share their riches liberally with each other, Jacob condemned the pride they had allowed to come into their lives along with wealth:

> And now, my brethren, I have spoken unto you concerning pride . . . because ye were proud in your hearts, of the things which God hath given you, what say ye of it?
>
> Do ye not suppose that such things are abominable unto him who created all flesh? And the one being is as precious in his sight as the other (Jacob 2:20–21).

As Jacob earlier explained, not only do those who are rich often pride themselves in their materially superior position to the poor, but they may actually grow to despise the poor: "But wo unto the rich, who are rich as to the things of the world. For because they are rich they despise the poor, and they persecute the meek" (2 Nephi 9:30).

President Ezra Taft Benson warned that the problem of pride is not just enmity between rich and poor but also enmity between the proud and God:

The central feature of pride is enmity—enmity toward God and toward our fellowmen. . . .

Our will in competition to God's will allows desires, appetites, and passions to go unbridled.[6]

Mormon alludes to this latter form of enmity in describing people who seemed especially pleased with themselves and their wealth: "But they grew proud, being lifted up in their hearts, because of their exceedingly great riches; therefore *they grew rich in their own eyes*" (Alma 45:24; emphasis added). Mormon's description of those who "grew rich in their own eyes" subtly mocks the notion that such individuals understand what it means to be truly wealthy. Such pride leads to a false sense of self-sufficiency, which the Lord sometimes corrects by leaving us on our own: "And because of this their great wickedness, and their boastings in their own strength," wrote Mormon later of another group of people who had fallen victim to their own prosperity, "*they were left in their own strength;* therefore they did not prosper, but were afflicted and smitten, and driven before the Lamanites, until they had lost possession of almost all their lands" (Helaman 4:13; emphasis added).

In sum, one of the greatest dangers of prosperity is that it makes us vulnerable to an infection of pride. The Book of Mormon documents in devastating detail how pride "had gotten into the hearts of the people; and it was because of their exceedingly great riches and their prosperity in the land; and it did grow upon them from day to day" (Helaman 3:36). Prosperity itself is not inherently evil; in fact, it is often the promised result of righteousness. But if we are to escape the heart disease of pride when we prosper, we must vigilantly guard against letting our prosperity lift us up in our own eyes. Perhaps the best preventive medicine against becoming infected with pride is, as discussed earlier, remembering "how merciful the Lord hath been" to us (Moroni 10:3) and being charitable toward the poor, as King Benjamin so forcefully urged his people (see Mosiah 4:16).

Their treasure became their god. It is possible, of course, to become wealthy without becoming proud. If we manage to avoid this particular pitfall, a second danger remains: enjoying what our money can buy so much that we become fixated on our earthly treasures. Jacob mentions this concern in the same breath with the problem of pride: "But wo unto the rich, who are rich as to the things of the world. For because they are rich they despise the poor, and they persecute the meek, and *their hearts are upon their treasures; wherefore, their treasure is their god*" (2 Nephi 9:30; emphasis added). King Noah "placed his heart upon his riches" (Mosiah 11:14), as did the wicked Jaredite king Jared, who "set his heart upon [his] kingdom and upon the glory of the world" (Ether 8:7). The tendency to yearn for the transient rewards of this earth is one of the characteristics of the natural man (see Mosiah 3:19). Thus, natural men and women easily fall prey to such lesser desires and are "quick to hearken unto the words of the evil one, and to set their hearts upon the vain things of the world!" (Helaman 12:4).

The source of the wind that blows us in this direction is also clear: "Now the cause of this iniquity of the people was this—Satan had great power, unto the stirring up of the people to do all manner of iniquity, and to the puffing them up with pride, tempting them to seek for power, and authority, and riches, and the vain things of the world" (3 Nephi 6:15). In his fictional depiction of devilish tactics, *The Screwtape Letters*, C. S. Lewis delightfully portrays how the adversary hopes to warm our hearts to things that don't matter so that we forget those things that do:

Prosperity knits a man to the World. He feels that he is "finding his place in it," while really it is finding its place in him. His increasing reputation, his widening circle of acquaintances, his sense of importance, the growing pressure of absorbing and agreeable work, build up in him a sense of being really at home in earth which is just what we want.[7]

Henry David Thoreau similarly commented on the potential that comfort and preoccupation with the wealth of this world have to distract us from the task of preparing ourselves for the next world: "We now no longer camp as for a night, but have settled down on earth and forgotten heaven. . . . We have built for this world a family mansion, and for the next a family tomb."[8]

Sadly, distraction can soon turn to corruption. In noting that King Mosiah had not succumbed to the consuming desires that typically overwhelm tyrants, Mormon refers to "that lucre which doth corrupt the soul" (Mosiah 29:40). Indeed, one of the problems in allowing our hearts to be swallowed up in a desire for the things of this world is that our values often become hostage to our carnal desires. Nephi, Lehi's brother, condemned those whose desires for material ends had become so ravenous that the people would do almost anything to satisfy their hunger for earthly treasure: "And ye have set your hearts upon the riches and the vain things of this world, for the which ye do murder, and plunder, and steal, and bear false witness against your neighbor, and do all manner of iniquity" (Helaman 7:21). The problem is not necessarily in *having* wealth (except as discussed further below), but in what we become willing to do or neglect in order to *obtain* wealth.

The dangers of lusting after riches are not limited to the wealthy. In Ether we read that Jared, the wicked king, "became exceedingly sorrowful because of the loss of the kingdom, for he had set his heart upon the kingdom and upon the glory of the world" (Ether 8:7). Such disappointment, of course, will be the final fate of all those who have set their hearts upon the things of this world when they eventually learn, as Alma taught his son, that we cannot carry these things with us (see Alma 39:14). But even those who only lust unsuccessfully after wealth can be distracted and corrupted by the mere quest. Thus, after condemning the wealthy who refuse to give of their substance to the poor (D&C 56:16), the Lord warned, "Wo [also] unto you poor men, . . . whose bellies are not satisfied, and whose hands are not stayed from laying hold upon other men's goods, whose eyes are full of greediness, and who will not labor with your own hands!" (D&C 56:17).

Be familiar with all and free with your substance. For true followers of Christ, who manage to prosper without becoming proud or preoccupied, one significant question remains: what do they do with their wealth? Jacob was the first prophet in the Book of Mormon to answer this question squarely. He challenged his people:

> Think of your brethren like unto yourselves, and be familiar with all and free with your substance, that they may be rich like unto you.
>
> But before ye seek for riches, seek ye for the kingdom of God.
>
> And after ye have obtained a hope in Christ ye shall obtain riches, if ye seek them; and ye will seek them for the intent to do good—to clothe the naked, and to feed the hungry, and to liberate the captive, and administer relief to the sick and the afflicted (Jacob 2:17–19).

Jacob first warned against the danger of preoccupation with wealth by cautioning his people to "seek for the kingdom of God" before they engage in their pursuit of riches. For Jacob, however, it was not enough that true followers of Christ remain spiritually grounded while obtaining wealth. Instead, he set the bar much higher in a statement that sounds almost more descriptive than prescriptive. When we seek the kingdom of God first and have truly "obtained a hope in Christ," there seems to be no question in Jacob's mind about the purpose for which our riches will be used: "ye will seek [riches] for the intent to do good—to clothe the naked, and to feed the hungry, and to liberate the captive, and administer relief to the sick and the afflicted" (Jacob 2:17–19).

Jacob's confidence about the ways spiritually grounded people will employ their riches illustrates clearly what he considers our obligations to be. King Benjamin articulated both those same expectations and a powerful rationale for them in his famous temple sermon. After encouraging his people to help those in need, including "the beggar," King Benjamin addressed potential objections to providing such assistance:

> Perhaps thou shalt say: The man has brought upon himself his misery; therefore I will stay my hand, . . . for his punishments are just—
>
> But I say unto you, O man, whosoever doeth this the same hath great cause to repent; and except he repenteth of that which he hath done he perisheth forever, and hath no interest in the kingdom of God.
>
> For behold, are we not all beggars? Do we not all depend upon the same Being, even God, for all the substance which we have, for both food and raiment, and for gold, and for silver, and for all the riches which we have of every kind? . . .
>
> And now, if God . . . doth grant unto you whatsoever ye ask that is right, . . . O then, how ye ought to impart of the substance that ye have one to another.
>
> And if ye judge the man who putteth up his petition to you for your substance. . . . , how much more just will be your condemnation

for withholding your substance, which doth not belong to you but to God, to whom also your life belongeth. . . .

I say unto you, wo be unto that man, for his substance shall perish with him; and now, I say these things unto those who are rich as pertaining to the things of this world (Mosiah 4:17–23).

In sum, according to King Benjamin, because God has been merciful and generous to us, we should mirror His mercy and generosity in our dealings with each other.[9]

Interestingly, the point of such philanthropy is not to ensure the rich become poor; instead, it was to help the poor become rich. The concern of Jacob and Benjamin was not necessarily with some individuals having too much, but with other individuals having too little. Jacob's charge was to "be familiar with all and free with your substance, that [your brethren] may be rich like unto you" (Jacob 2:17). The root for the word *familiar* is the same as the root for the word *family,* and the primary meaning for the term from the 1828 Webster's Dictionary is "pertaining to a family, domestic." In other words, Jacob expected those blessed with wealth to treat the less fortunate as if they were family.

The righteous members of the Church during Alma the Younger's day did just this with their "abundance" of everything from flocks and herds to grain to gold and silver. In their "prosperous circumstances," they were careful not to send away anyone in need. Nor did they "set their hearts upon riches." Instead, "they were liberal to all," including those who were not members of the Church. Paradoxically, their very generosity led them to prosper even more (see Alma 1:29–31).

Of course, in a community or society with relatively few poor to lift out of poverty, it is easier for the rich to share without giving up all their wealth. However, in a globally connected world, the resources of the righteous rich may well not be enough to lift everyone out of poverty while still leaving the once rich with an abundance. Under such circumstances, King Benjamin's advice would probably be for those who have more than they need to do what they prudently can to help those who have not—without undermining their ability to provide for their own families' needs: "And see that all these things are done in wisdom and order; for it is not requisite that a man should run faster than he has strength" (Mosiah 4:27). Elder Dallin H. Oaks echoed this important caution about prudence when he warned:

> We are commanded to give to the poor. Could the fulfillment of that fundamental Christian obligation be carried to excess? I believe it can. I have seen cases in which persons fulfilled that duty to such an extent that they impoverished their own families by expending resources of property or time that were needed for family members.[10]

Following the Savior's appearance to the descendants of Lehi, the Saints managed to reach a remarkable level of consecration without impoverishing themselves. Instead of giving away everything so that they became poor, the rich apparently gave away enough that the poor were no longer poor and the rich were no longer rich. Instead, everyone had enough, with "all things common among them; therefore there were not rich and poor, bond and free, but they were all made free, and partakers of the heavenly gift" (4 Nephi 1:3). Indeed, such conditions of compassion and unity constitute part of the very definition of a Zion people: "And the Lord called his people Zion, because they were of one heart and one mind, and dwelt in righteousness; and there was no poor among them" (Moses 7:18). Though the precise mechanics of the Lord's welfare system may fluctuate,[11] his overall expectations of how we will use riches (should we reap them) seems clear: we will help those in need, striving to lift all those we can out of poverty.[12]

THE TRANSITORY NATURE OF WEALTH

One antidote to the three primary pitfalls of prosperity—pride, preoccupation, and failing to help those in poverty—is to remember the transitory nature of wealth. In counseling his son to "seek not after riches nor the vain things of this world," Alma the Younger reasoned with Corianton: "for behold, you cannot carry them with you" (Alma 39:14). If worldly riches, unlike knowledge and intelligence, do not rise with us in the resurrection (see D&C 130:18–19), then what is the point in hoarding them, setting our hearts on them, or thinking of ourselves as better than others because we have obtained them? Alma imparts just such eternal perspective by reminding his son and us that we cannot carry the riches or vain things of this world with us when we die.

The Lord makes a similar point with a haunting object lesson during the darkest points of Nephite society. Samuel the Lamanite prophesied that those who rejected the prophets would have great difficulty retaining their earthly possessions:

> And behold, the time cometh that he curseth *your riches,* that they *become slippery, that ye cannot hold them;* and in the days of your poverty ye cannot retain them.
>
> . . . And then shall ye lament, and say:
>
> . . . O that we had remembered the Lord our God in the day that he gave us *our riches,* and then they would not *have become slippery* that we should lose them; for behold, *our riches are gone from us. . . .*
>
> Yea, we have hid up our treasures and they have slipped away from us, because of the curse of the land.
>
> O that we had repented in the day that the word of the Lord came unto us; for behold the land is cursed, and *all things are become slippery, and we cannot hold them* (Helaman 13:31–36; emphasis added).

We read of the fulfillment of Samuel's prophecy in Mormon 1:18, when the Gadianton robbers "did infest the land, insomuch that the inhabitants thereof began to hide up their treasures in the earth; and *they became slippery,* because the Lord had cursed the land, that *they could not hold them, nor retain them again*" (emphasis added). This prophecy and its fulfillment were literal: people were physically unable to hold on to their treasures. Yet this phenomenon is also marvelously symbolic of the transitory nature of material wealth, which is destined to slip through our fingers, leaving us empty if we have not laid up (spiritual) treasures for ourselves in heaven (see 3 Nephi 13:20). Conversely, those who follow the prophets will be able to carry their riches with them, because the riches they accumulate will last eternally (see D&C 11:7).

THEREFORE, WHAT?

Writing this chapter was probably a terrible tactical mistake. My wife reminds me of it every time I want to engage in what I think President Spencer W. Kimball had in mind when he spoke of "reasonable luxuries."[13] My track record is far from perfect, but my hope is that I have better handled what prosperity we have enjoyed by consciously considering the teachings of Book of Mormon writers. These uniquely positioned prophets and seers saw the pride pattern in history and glimpsed the materialistic focus of our day. If nothing else, they have given us a marvelous framework for deciding what to do with our wealth and for avoiding its pitfalls.

The framework is more complicated than simply not seeking wealth, since even those who follow Alma's counsel on that point (see Alma 39:14) may still end up prospering. Indeed, those who follow God's prophets, including their counsel to work hard and not be slothful (see D&C 58:26–27; 88:123–24), are prone to prosper. Both Jacob and King Benjamin assume that many followers of Christ will attain riches and will liberally share their wealth to help those less fortunate (see Jacob 2:17–18; Mosiah 4:11–12, 16–23). Rather than moving to a monastery, prosperous followers of Christ who prayerfully strive to observe prophetic parameters in the use and distribution of their means will find ways to successfully navigate the hazards of prosperity.

When I was a BYU student, a professor whom I greatly respected was once talking with a group of students in his home about these issues. As he spoke about the need to use our means to help those less fortunate than us, I noticed that he had a piano in his home. It was modest but still must have cost well over a thousand dollars. Being more impudent than insightful, I asked him about the propriety of owning a piano when there were so many people in the world who couldn't afford to eat.

Treating me with more respect than I deserved, he replied, in effect, "That's a good question. I can't tell you for sure that we made the right decision in doing that, but I can tell you that we thought about it and even prayed about whether the Lord would have us make that purchase. For our family, we felt like it was the right thing to do."

His humility and thoughtfulness taught me an important lesson. His family's motive in purchasing the piano was not to impress others or make themselves feel better than others. Instead, it was to enable their children to learn about music and to bring music into their home. The family did not boast about their piano or seem preoccupied with it, nor did the purchase appear to stretch them beyond their financial limits. Finally, this professor and his wife had prayed about whether the Lord approved that particular major acquisition at that time in their lives. Given his attitude, I believe he and his family would have forgone the purchase and even given the funds to others in greater need had the Lord so prompted him.

Scrutinizing our motives and seeking direction from the Lord can help the prosperous be vigilant against the dangers of wealth about which Book of Mormon prophets warned. Personalizing the process can also help us refrain from judging others who have chosen to use their riches differently than we have. Because of differences in our abilities, our future circumstances, and even our current circumstances, Heavenly Father may prompt individuals who seem to be in the same financial situation to make very different decisions about what things to buy or what jobs to take. One family with excess funds might be prompted to add to their savings account as a stay against future economic difficulties; another family might be prompted to buy a boat because it will be the only thing that keeps a teenage child close to them during a rebellious period; yet another family might be prompted to dramatically increase their contributions to the Perpetual Education Fund. When we are tempted to assess someone else's righteousness (with regard to finances or anything else), we would do well to leave those judgments to Him who knows all things.

Though the Book of Mormon's teachings on riches do not give us license to judge others, they do give us some great guidance for judging how to use our *own* earthly riches. In sum, here's the checklist:

- We are to guard against letting worldly success give us an inflated view of ourselves—in relation either to others or to God.
- Whether we are rich or hoping to be rich, we are to avoid setting our hearts on riches and other vain things of the world because such treasures and honors cannot be carried with us (see Alma 39:14).

- Finally, to the extent we are blessed with an abundance of material things, we will remember the Source of our bounty and emulate His generosity toward us in sharing liberally with His children who are in need.

LESSONS ON
GOD'S GUIDANCE

SWIMMING WITHOUT LANES

The word of God provides us a saving standard we need more than we might think.

In contrast to my father and older sister, I have never considered myself a natural swimmer. So when a bishop at college coaxed me into participating in a couple of mini-triathlons, swimming was by far the most difficult part of my training regimen. But after months of practice in the college pool and complete humiliation in my first mini-triathlon, I went from being a very slow swimmer to being an almost average swimmer—a moral victory, of sorts. When I returned home from school, I was eager to pit my newfound skills against my father and sister, hopeful that I could finally beat them in a race.

We decided to hold a family biathlon, with a swimming leg and a running leg. The venue was a beautiful state park with a trail encircling a lake. My father, my sister, and I were the contestants in the swimming segment, which began at a dock on one side of the lake and ended at a beach on the other, where we were to tag the runners. As soon as the signal was given, I burst from the dock, churning my arms furiously. Soon I could see neither my father nor my sister, who had not been training for mini-triathlons. I was rather pleased with myself—until I heard my sister's voice calling out to me. Much more compassionate and less competitive than I, she had stopped swimming long enough to alert me to a very disappointing and embarrassing fact: while she and my father were headed directly for the beach that was our target, I had veered off at roughly a 45-degree angle from our destination.

I eventually arrived at the beach and tagged my partner, humbled and puzzled. In all my practice and in the two mini-triathlons in which I had competed, I had never had any trouble staying on course. Why now? The answer proved to be fairly simple: I had always swum in pools with ropes that divided the lanes. I had hardly noticed the ropes; I certainly hadn't thought I needed them. Obviously, it turned out that I was quite wrong. Without the constraining help of those lanes, especially under the pressure of a race, my natural tendency was to swim a very crooked course.

Just as swimming in a lake allowed me to discover how much I needed swimming lanes, the experience of Lehi and his descendants demonstrates the importance of the written word of God in our lives. After Nephi had succeeded in obtaining the brass plates from Laban, Lehi and his faithful son "searched [the records] and found that they were desirable; yea, even of great worth unto us, insomuch that we could preserve the commandments of the Lord unto our children" (1 Nephi 5:21).

"BETTER THAT ONE MAN SHOULD PERISH"

As Nephi hovered over the drunken Laban and puzzled over the Spirit's prompting to kill the possessor of the brass plates, the Holy Ghost provided Nephi with several rationales justifying the act.[1] The Spirit declared that a terrible fate awaited Lehi's descendants if they did not obtain the brass plates containing God's commandments: "It is better that one man should perish than that a nation should dwindle and perish in unbelief." Nephi then remembered the Lord's earlier promise: "Inasmuch as thy seed shall keep my commandments, they shall prosper in the land of promise." Upon reflection, Nephi realized the connection between the promise of prosperity and the Spirit's prediction that Lehi's seed would dwindle and perish in unbelief without the brass plates. He understood that his people "could not keep the commandments of the Lord according to the law of Moses, save they should have the law," which Nephi already knew was "engraven upon the plates of brass." The deductive logic was simple: if no brass plates, then no memory of the law; if no memory of the law, then no belief in or obedience to the law; if disbelief in and disobedience to the law, then destruction. Convinced, Nephi "did obey the voice of the Spirit" and killed Laban—a rather gruesome object lesson to Nephi and his family on just how important it was for them to have the scriptures (see 1 Nephi 4:13–18).

Certainly having access to the written word of God is beneficial, but the prediction made by the Spirit was sweeping and dire: without the brass plates, an entire "nation [would] dwindle and perish in unbelief." Surely the scriptures are helpful, but couldn't the Nephites have preserved righteous traditions orally? The Mulekites' experience answers this question, providing the experimental group to Lehi's control group in what amounts to a macro case study with the word of God.

THE MULEKITES SWIM WITHOUT LANES

We do not know much about the Mulekites, whose exodus from the Old World to the New World is not nearly as well documented as that of the Jaredites or Lehi's family. (Such lack of detail is hardly surprising, given the lack of a record among the Mulekites.) Named after Mulek, a surviving son of King Zedekiah who was among their party (see Mosiah 25:2; Helaman 8:21), the Mulekites fled Jerusalem when

Zedekiah was "carried away captive into Babylon" (Omni 1:15), shortly after the departure of Lehi's family. The Nephite record makes no mention of them until more than three centuries after both parties' arrival in the New World, when the Nephites were again forced to flee the Lamanites and find a new homeland. Led by the righteous King Mosiah I (Benjamin's father), the Nephites discovered a land called Zarahemla, populated by their distant Israelite cousins, the Mulekites.

Like the Nephites, the Mulekites had endured "many wars and serious contentions." Unlike the Nephites, "their language had become corrupted; and they had brought no records with them." Most significantly, the Mulekites "denied the being of their Creator" (Omni 1:17). Without the help of a scriptural account among them, these Israelites had declined into spiritual ignorance. Fortunately, they responded well to the mass emigration of the Nephites, learning their language and rejoicing "exceedingly, because the Lord had sent the people of Mosiah with the plates of brass which contained the record of the Jews" (Omni 1:14; see also verse 18).

KING BENJAMIN'S SPIRITUAL LITERACY DRIVE

Whether or not King Benjamin was old enough to witness the Mulekites' spiritual illiteracy firsthand, he must have at least been taught about their experience by his father, Mosiah I, who discovered the Mulekites in Zarahemla. Moreover, as Nephite and Mulekite societies integrated, especially just one generation after their merger, the ruler of this new combined people would have been intimately familiar with the lingering effects of the Mulekites' multi-generational deficiency of scripture study. After all, these Israelite cousins of the Nephites formed a major part of Benjamin's kingdom; when a census was taken a generation later during the reign of his son, Mosiah II, there were more Mulekites than Nephites (see Mosiah 25:2).

If Nephi's conversation with the Spirit served as a prologue to the great scripture study experiment, King Benjamin's counsel to his sons about the importance of scripture study is the epilogue. Just a generation after seeing exactly what happened to a group of Israelites who left Jerusalem without the benefit of a written record, Benjamin ensured that his sons were "taught in all the language of his fathers" (Mosiah 1:2). The purpose of this academic training was to help Benjamin's boys "become men of understanding" who would "know concerning the prophecies which had been spoken by the mouths of their fathers" (Mosiah 1:2).[2] King Benjamin taught his sons about the importance of the plates of brass, in particular: "My sons, I would that ye should remember that were it not for these plates, which contain these records and these commandments, we must have suffered in ignorance, even at this present time, not knowing the mysteries of God" (Mosiah 1:3).

Because we do not know much about the spiritual beginnings of the Mulekites, it is fair to ask whether Lehi's party might not have stood a better chance of staying on the strait and narrow path than the Mulekites did, even if Lehi's people had not brought a record with them. Whether they would have taken longer to stray is unclear, but King Benjamin concurs with the Spirit's conclusion in 1 Nephi 4:13: without the plates, even Lehi's descendants would have gone astray. One practical reason is the difficulty of remembering the commandments in their pure form without some written[3] standard:

> For it were not possible that our father, Lehi, could have remembered all these things,[4] to have taught them to his children, except it were for the help of these plates. . . .
>
> I say unto you, my sons, were it not for these things, which have been kept and preserved by the hand of God, that we might read and understand of his mysteries, and have his commandments always

before our eyes, that *even our fathers would have dwindled in unbelief* (Mosiah 1:4–5; emphasis added).

King Benjamin echoes the wording of the Spirit when he concludes that even his fathers "would have dwindled in unbelief" without the plates for which Nephi killed. Then, just as Nephi realized his people could not keep the commandments and prosper if they did not have the commandments (see 1 Nephi 4:14–15), King Benjamin counseled his sons to study the scriptures diligently so that they could prosper: "And now, my sons, I would that ye should remember to search them diligently, that ye may profit thereby; and I would that ye should keep the commandments of God, that ye may prosper in the land according to the promises which the Lord made unto our fathers" (Mosiah 1:7).

ENLARGING THE MEMORY

Speaking of the plates of brass and of the record kept by his Nephite forefathers, Alma told his son Helaman that "they have enlarged the memory of this people" (Alma 37:8). If those who do not learn from history generally are destined to repeat the mistakes of the past, the same is certainly true for those who do not learn from the past spiritually. Comparing the respective fates of the Nephites and Mulekites is but one example of how the scriptural record allows us to learn from the spiritual mistakes and successes of those who have gone before, motivating us to repeat the successes and avoid duplicating the mistakes. As Elder Neal A. Maxwell has observed, "Searched and 'likened' to ourselves effectively, the scriptures can thereby '[enlarge] the memory of this people' (see Alma 37:8), emancipating us from the limitations of our own time and place; the spiritual database is expanded. If we are meek, the case studies in the scriptures help us to see our own case more clearly."[5]

Furthermore, as we look back on millennia of humankind's experience with God, such scriptural perspective sometimes makes it easier to recognize "how merciful the Lord hath been unto the children of men, from the creation of Adam even down until" the present day (Moroni 10:3). When we begin to forget just how forgiving and full of grace God has been to us individually and to His people historically, scripture study provides the antidote to such spiritual Alzheimer's.

THEREFORE, WHAT?

It is easy to underestimate our need for the constant guidance that comes from daily studying the word of God. Feeling that past scripture study has pointed us in the right direction already, we may believe that we can continue our swim without the further aid of lanes or standards. My swimming analogy would be even more fitting, however, if I'd been swimming across a saltwater harbor, which would have added swirling undercurrents and ebbing and flowing tides to my naturally erratic stroke. In real life, we battle not only the natural man, but powerful tides of temptation. To combat these ongoing problems, past scripture study simply isn't sufficient to give us the strength we need to combat current challenges. As President Ezra Taft Benson put it, "Yesterday's meal is not enough to sustain today's needs. So also an infrequent reading of 'the most correct of any book on earth,' as Joseph Smith called it, is not enough."[6]

Allow me to illustrate with a simple example. In the alumni magazine of the law school I attended, there is a section providing an update on the accomplishments of my classmates and other graduates. When I begin reading about the professional heights to which others have climbed, I sometimes find myself comparing their achievements with my own, perhaps even yearning to experience what they have experienced, even though such accomplishments often require significant sacrifices of family time. On the other hand, when I study the scriptures, such worldly pulls and tugs are replaced with far better heroes, whose feats of faith inspire me instead. In the process, my memory of what really matters is refreshed; my spiritual data bank is expanded.

For me, the lesson of these Book of Mormon teachings is that I must study God's word daily to keep myself from drifting off course. Remembering the price these prophets paid to obtain and produce the scriptures in their day helps me cherish it more in ours. Having killed a man at God's command to obtain the sacred record, Nephi probably did not let the plates of brass gather dust, unused, after an initial reading or two. His graphic object lesson undoubtedly reminded him and should remind us that without regular nourishment from the "good word of God" (Moroni 6:4), we will all perish spiritually.

NOT OF MYSELF BUT OF GOD

—◦—

Like Paul, Alma emphasized the importance of receiving a confirmation
of spiritual truths through spiritual means.

When interviewing youth as a bishop, I discovered many who
believed the Church was true but who hadn't obtained a spiritual testimony. "Why do you believe the Church is true?" I would ask,
seeking to determine the depth of their testimony.

"Well," replied one very young man, "the Book of Mormon, it's
just so thick—it has to be true." I was grateful he had not yet met anyone from another faith with a thicker book.

Alma the Younger's intellectual testimony of the gospel was far
firmer than the suppositions of these youth or even those who lean
upon the more sophisticated archeological or linguistic evidence avail-
able to us today: Alma had experienced an earth-shaking, life-
changing angelic visitation with his own senses. Yet when Alma later
testified of the truthfulness of the principles he preached, he placed
less weight on this dramatic physical event than on the witness he had
obtained from the Holy Ghost. Alma's example teaches us that though
intellectual evidence may help jumpstart our testimonies, we must
ultimately obtain our own *spiritual* witness if we are to fully embrace
the gospel.

"HOW DO YE SUPPOSE THAT I KNOW?"

Toward the end of his searing sermon to the lukewarm members in Zarahemla, Alma bore a powerful testimony. But it was not enough for him to tell his listeners that he knew; Alma wanted to make sure they understood *how* he knew. He asked them, "And how do ye suppose that I know of their surety?" (Alma 5:45).

For some, the answer must have seemed obvious. Alma knew of the surety of these things because he had seen an angel, face to face. Such an experience would seem to be particularly compelling evidence to quiet a rather skeptical crowd. But as Alma explained how he knew, he did not even mention his miraculous encounter with a heavenly being:

> Behold, I say unto you they are made known unto me by the Holy Spirit of God. Behold, I have fasted and prayed many days that I might know these things of myself. And now I do know of myself that they are true; for the Lord God hath made them manifest unto me by his Holy Spirit; and this is the spirit of revelation which is in me (Alma 5:46).

To most, Alma's extraordinary revelation would seem more compelling evidence than the promptings of the Holy Ghost. Even short of angelic visitations, Alma could have invoked other proofs for the truthfulness of his message. From his articulate and profound discourses, it's clear that Alma was highly intelligent.[1] He undoubtedly appreciated the many powerful logical evidences of the truthfulness of the gospel. But in Zarahemla Alma does not cite these as the reason he knows. Instead, he points to the same source through which Moroni promised the truth of all things could be known—the Holy Ghost (see Moroni 10:5; Alma 5:46–47).

In his later, private farewell teachings to his sons Helaman and

Shiblon, Alma did mention the visitation of the angel as part of his testimony. However, he described that visitation only after stating that he had learned the spiritual truths in question through the Holy Ghost. Alma is emphatic in identifying the ultimate source of his knowledge as spiritual (i.e., God-given) rather than secular (i.e., humanly derived):

> And I would not that ye think that I know of myself—not of the temporal but of the spiritual, not of the carnal mind but of God. . . .
>
> I would not that ye should think that I know these things of myself, but it is the Spirit of God which is in me which maketh these things known unto me (Alma 36:4; 38:6).

Alma wanted to be as clear with his sons as he had been with the members in Zarahemla: his knowledge of the eternal truths of the gospel stemmed not from any mortal mathematics he had performed to deduce these things, but from the power of God and His Spirit, which had testified to Alma's soul. What Alma teaches us is that a true testimony is obtained by a spiritual confirmation rather than from an acquired set of conclusions reached through rational exercise or even an angelic visitation.

SPIRITUAL MEANS FOR LEARNING SPIRITUAL TRUTHS

Alma's failure to mention his angelic visitation to the saints in Zarahemla calls to mind a statement by President Joseph Fielding Smith:

> A visitation of an angel, a tangible resurrected being, would not leave the impression and would not convince us and place within us that *something which we cannot get away from which we receive through a manifestation of the Holy Ghost.* Personal visitations might

become dim as time goes on, but this guidance of the Holy Ghost is renewed and continued, day after day, year after year, if we live to be worthy of it.[2]

As Laman and Lemuel's experiences demonstrate, the effects of angelic visitations alone can be fleeting; no sooner had their angel departed than Nephi's brothers resumed their murmuring (see 1 Nephi 3:31). A confirmation of truth from the Holy Ghost, on the other hand, sears within our hearts "something which we cannot get away from." Like spiritual oatmeal, promptings of the Spirit stay with us. On the other hand, convictions based solely on intellectual or physical evidence may satisfy our immediate appetite but cannot provide lasting sustenance. Thus, Alma emphasizes obtaining confirmation of spiritual truths through spiritual means, even if we have already arrived at the same conclusions through some compelling physical or intellectual evidence. Nothing underscores this point more clearly than his declaration that after seeing the angel, he "fasted and prayed many days that [he] might know these things" (Alma 5:46).[3]

In answer to his fasting and prayer, Alma obtained his witness: "I say unto you that it has thus been revealed unto me, that the words which have been spoken by our fathers are true, even so according to the spirit of prophecy which is in me, which is also by the manifestation of the Spirit of God" (Alma 5:47). Joseph Smith taught that this is the only way we can know of the ultimate truth in the gospel plan: "No man can *know* that Jesus is the Lord, but by the Holy Ghost" (emphasis added).[4] However compelling other evidence of the Savior's divinity may be, true knowledge of this and other gospel truths comes only through the Holy Ghost.

"TO BE LEARNED IS GOOD"

None of this should lead us to view intellectual learning as undesirable. To the contrary, Jacob reminds us that "to be learned is good"—if we can manage to keep our pride in check and continue to "hearken unto the counsels of God" (2 Nephi 9:29). Moreover, honest intellectual effort on our part often precedes the blessing we really seek—knowledge from God.[5] The testimonies of the witnesses printed in the front of the Book of Mormon demonstrate that intellectual evidence sometimes plays a role in the process of learning truth. And though Alma's testimony ultimately came from the Holy Ghost, the shock and awe of seeing an angel gave him a much-needed spiritual wake-up call. Thus, Elder Dallin H. Oaks notes, "Intellectual things—reason and logic—can prepare the way, and they can help us in our preparation."[6] God mercifully gives some fairly impressive intellectual evidence as an appetizer to those who are deciding whether to undertake a serious spiritual inquiry for their main course.

The trick is simply to make sure we don't let the appetizer become the whole meal. If we become so comfortable with intellectual convictions (including correct ones) that we never take the next step of seeking divine confirmation of spiritual truths, we deprive ourselves of the spiritual sustenance necessary to nourish us in difficult times.

Elder Henry B. Eyring described some of the dangers of moving forward based solely on intellectual evidence in this way:

> It is helpful to meet a brilliant mind who defends gospel truths with fact and logic. There is comfort in finding that such a person has confronted the same questions with which you struggle and has retained his faith. But there is a hazard. Even the most brilliant and faithful person may defend the truth with argument or fact that later proves false. The best scholarship has, at least, incompleteness in it. But even flawless argument has a weakness if you come to depend on

it: What happens to the next doubt, or the next? What if no physical evidence or persuasive logic can be produced to dispel it? You will find then what I have found—that faithful scholar who reassured you with logic did not base his faith there.[7]

Just as undiscovered faulty brakes give drivers a false sense of security, a purely intellectual conviction that the gospel is true can give us a false sense of spiritual security. No matter how well reasoned, such "knowledge" will not weather the inevitable storms of doubt in the same way as testimonies built upon the rock of revelation.[8] As compelling as the intellectual case is for the gospel's truthfulness, in the final analysis purely secular evidence is no match, for example, for the argument that resurrection is scientifically impossible—or dozens of other intellectual challenges Satan will pose to our testimonies.

THEREFORE, WHAT?

Alma the Younger is emphatic about making sure his sons and the Nephite saints understand that his knowledge comes from the Holy Ghost rather than from himself. For me, that realization prompts me to do at least three things:

- make sure my own testimony is grounded in revelation rather than mere reason;
- help move my children and others for whom I have stewardship along the spectrum from a working intellectual assumption to actual spiritual knowledge; and
- when teaching the gospel to others inside and outside the Church, be careful not to cite as evidence the "wisdom of men" instead of the "wisdom of God" (see 1 Corinthians 2:4–5, 10–14).

Sometimes when I encounter the skepticism of friends, students, children, or even myself, I'm inclined to lean first on intellectual "proofs" to support our beliefs. It's not hard to find compelling evidence and logical conclusions to support gospel principles and sacred events; after all, the things we teach are true. In fact, for many who have been or are being raised in the restored gospel, the evidence of its truthfulness can be so overwhelming that it may seem to render the case closed, without the need for any further spiritual inquiry.

For example, the sudden emergence of the Book of Mormon—complete with its doctrinal sophistication, ancient Near Eastern poetry, remarkable array of names, and variety of writing styles—is powerfully persuasive evidence of the truthfulness of Joseph Smith's claims about its origins. Comfortable with that pile of facts on our side, we may coast along without seeking a spiritual witness of the book's truthfulness. Alma reminds me that a conviction based on intellectual evidence or arguments is not enough, for me or my children or anyone else I hope to bring unto Christ.

As a teenager, I came to understand this important principle through painful trial and error. Growing up in the Seattle area, I had many friends who were not members of the Church. However, they all belonged to some Christian faith and had an active interest in religion, leading to many lively discussions about our respective beliefs. Our friendship spared our exchanges from the acrimony that characterizes most "bashing," but the principal mode of persuasion was unquestionably intellectual. I answered scriptures with scriptures and questions with diplomatic, logical explanations, often beginning with the softening phrase, "We believe. . . ." By the time we were seniors in high school, my friends respected my religious beliefs and understood them, but not as well as I thought.

Shortly before we parted ways for college, an inspired ward

missionary (then a seventy) challenged me to invite some friends to my home to have the missionaries share the gospel. Frankly, I bristled a bit, feeling that I had been doing this on my own for at least four years. But the Spirit softened my heart, and another LDS friend and I eventually invited four friends to my home, along with the missionaries. The discussion that evening proved to be different from any previous gospel discussion we had had.

The missionaries set a marvelous tone as they bore their testimonies and explained some of the basic principles of the gospel. My LDS friend and I then did something I had never previously done with these friends: we bore testimony, beginning with "I *know* . . ." Opening up and sharing what I felt and had come to know through the Spirit was difficult; I felt much more vulnerable than when I'd offered more diplomatic, encyclopedia-style explanations of our beliefs. As I shared my convictions, I cried—not something 18-year-old young men are eager to do in front of friends. Yet the Spirit attended to our discussion in a way it had never blessed my previous intellectually-based attempts to teach the gospel.

None of my friends joined the Church, but they all felt something they had not felt before. After the discussion was over, one of them asked if we could step outside for a moment. "Rob, I never knew how you felt," my friend explained, to my amazement. Despite hours of earnest scriptural discussions, I had failed to convey the depth of my spiritual convictions to my friend. Although none of my friends was baptized, statements they made about that night made it clear to me that they had felt the Spirit, which had affected them in a fundamentally deeper and different way than hours of earnest intellectual discussion ever had.

Never again would I try to teach the gospel solely with "the enticing of man's wisdom" (see 1 Corinthians 2:4–5). Instead, I have striven to teach "the word of truth by the Comforter, in the Spirit of truth" rather than "some other way" (D&C 50:17–18; cf. D&C 42:14).

Physical evidence and rational persuasion can certainly play a role in our search for spiritual truth. But if we hope to provide our skeptics, our children, our students, or ourselves with lasting knowledge of the truthfulness of spiritual claims primarily through temporal means alone, we will be disappointed. If intellectual analysis does not eventually lead to spiritual inquiry, it cannot yield spiritual knowledge.[9] To know as Alma knew, we must seek and obtain confirmation of spiritual truths as Alma did: from God, through the Holy Ghost.

LESSONS ON

LEADERSHIP

PLAYING TO SMALL CROWDS

Some of the greatest prophets ministered to small congregations,
yet their impact on the world was great.

Lehi, Nephi, Jacob, and Abinadi are among the most remarkable prophets whose teachings we find in the Book of Mormon. Through their writings and examples, these four prophets have become household names in literally millions of homes in our day. Such modern fame may lead us to overlook one somewhat surprising aspect of their mortal ministries: these prophets played almost exclusively to small crowds. From their example, we learn how important it is to magnify our callings, whatever the number of people we are called to serve.

SMALL CROWDS

Lehi began his ministry preaching in the relatively large venue of Jerusalem (see 1 Nephi 1:4, 18), but he was essentially booed off the stage (1 Nephi 1:20).[1] When the tomatoes became stones, the Lord warned Lehi and his family to flee (1 Nephi 1:20; 1 Nephi 2:1–2). Suddenly, Lehi's priesthood responsibilities changed from being a big city prophet to serving almost exclusively as a family patriarch. Although there is some speculation about nomadic groups Lehi may have proselytized during his years in the wilderness, for the rest of his life, Lehi's ministry consisted largely of teaching his family, Ishmael's family, and Zoram. His teachings that we have come to cherish are essentially the transcripts of some remarkable family councils and family home evenings (see, for example, 1 Nephi 8, 2 Nephi 2).

As Lehi's descendants proliferated, the size of the congregation increased, but in all likelihood Lehi's sons Nephi and Jacob taught dozens rather than hundreds of people (and certainly not thousands). In essence, their ministry was to siblings, children, grandchildren, and, perhaps by the end of their lives, great-grandchildren. While we cannot completely rule out the possibility that the Nephites encountered other inhabitants of the New World during the lifetimes of Nephi and Jacob, Jacob's own epilogue to his life suggests his acquaintances consisted of his exiled family: "The time passed away with us, and also our lives passed away like as it were unto us a dream, we being a lonesome and a solemn people, wanderers, cast out from Jerusalem, born in tribulation, in a wilderness, and hated of our brethren" (Jacob 7:26).

Centuries later the Lord sent Abinadi, a courageous prophet and extraordinary teacher, to preach to the inhabitants of the two reclaimed Nephite outposts of Lehi-Nephi and Shilom. Like Lehi's in Jerusalem, Abinadi's reception was less than warm: the people "were wroth with him, and sought to take away his life" (Mosiah 11:26). We do not know whether Abinadi's labors included preaching to other people in other cities, but from what we do know of his life, it seems that he did not have the privilege of speaking to any kind of congregation of believers. Some might have even called his mission a failure because it resulted in the conversion of only one person of whom we know.[2]

BIG IMPACTS

Despite the relatively small size of their congregations and stewardships during their lifetimes, each of these prophets has had an incredibly large impact on the lives of untold numbers of people. Lehi's vision of the tree of life alone, for example, has been a vivid and powerful metaphor for millions of readers of the Book of Mormon. His teachings about the Fall and the Atonement, together with those of his son, Jacob (who was clearly influenced by his father's instruction), provide us with some of the most powerful and instructive writings in all of scripture on these subjects (see 2 Nephi 2, 6, 9). And it is through Nephi's diligent record keeping that we have access to most of these visions and doctrines. Finally, Nephi's own example of courageous obedience in obtaining the brass plates, making a new bow, and building a ship to cross the great deep have appropriately become the stuff of Primary songs, now embedded in the memories of millions of Latter-day Saint children. Nephi may have been viewed as a protector and beloved leader by some of his siblings and their descendants in his day (see Jacob 1:10), but he is viewed as a hero by millions in our day.

Interestingly, the writings of First and Second Nephi may not have been widely read by Lehi's descendants before our day. Only after Mormon abridged the large plates of Nephi with their secular history (see 1 Nephi 9:2) does he note, "I searched among the records which had been delivered into my hands, and I found these plates, which contained this small account of the prophets, from Jacob down to the reign of this king Benjamin, and also many of the words of Nephi" (Words of Mormon 1:3). Mormon was delighted with his find: "And the things which are upon these plates pleasing me, because of the prophecies of the coming of Christ; . . . [w]herefore, I chose these things, to finish my record upon them . . . for they are choice unto me; and I know they will be choice unto my brethren" (Words of Mormon 1:4–6).

Thus, it appears that even the compiler of the Book of Mormon himself did not have the privilege of reading 1 Nephi, 2 Nephi, and Jacob until near the end of his life (see Words of Mormon 1:1). Exactly when these plates became lost amid the prolific pile of Nephite records is not clear, but the fact that Mormon writes of finding them could explain a curious statement by Alma the Younger. Speaking of the Messiah who was to come, Alma wrote, "I do not say that he will come among us at the time of his dwelling in his mortal tabernacle; for behold, the Spirit hath not said unto me that this should be the case" (Alma 7:8). Such a statement seems odd in light of Nephi's vision in 1 Nephi 12, in which he plainly saw his own seed and the seed of his brethren (1 Nephi 12:1), the terrible destruction and darkness that would occur 600 years later (1 Nephi 12:4–5), and "the heavens open, and the Lamb of God descending out of heaven; and he came down and showed himself unto them" (1 Nephi 12:6). If it sounds as if Alma hadn't read 1 Nephi, it may be because he hadn't.

In any event, Nephi, Jacob, Mormon, and Moroni wrote not so much for their contemporaries or even their immediate descendants but "for our day," taught President Ezra Taft Benson. "The Nephites never had the book; neither did the Lamanites of ancient times. It was meant for us."[3] Thus, the greatest impact of these prophets' writings came not even a generation or two later, but a millennium or two later.

Abinadi's impact was also delayed but profound. It is sheer speculation, but I like to think that as he taught King Noah's apostate priests, the Spirit might have prompted Abinadi to know that one of them would receive his message and carry it forward. Perhaps he even had his eye on a trembling, remorseful Alma when he concluded his sermon with a call not only to repentance, but to teach:

PLAYING TO SMALL CROWDS

And now, ought ye not to tremble and repent of your sins, and remember that only in and through Christ ye can be saved?

Therefore, if ye teach the law of Moses, also teach that it is a shadow of those things which are to come—

Teach them that redemption cometh through Christ the Lord, who is the very Eternal Father. Amen (Mosiah 16:13–15).

Whether or not Abinadi had a premonition of the impact of his words, the fact is that "there was one among them whose name was Alma, . . . a young man, and he believed the words which Abinadi had spoken" (Mosiah 17:2). As a former member of King Noah's corrupt power structure, Alma later witnessed, he had been "caught in a snare, and did many things which were abominable in the sight of the Lord," causing him "sore repentance" (Mosiah 23:9). Pricked by Abinadi's stirring sermon, the young priest pled for mercy for Abinadi—promptly losing his job and nearly losing his head (see Mosiah 17:2–3).

In hiding, the first thing he did was "write all the words which Abinadi had spoken" (Mosiah 17:4). We are thus indebted to Alma for the marvelous account we have of Abinadi's unflinching courage and incredible sermon. Soon Alma began to "teach the words of Abinadi" (Mosiah 18:1) to those brave souls who would listen. By the time King Noah's army forced Alma's "ward" to flee, 204 souls had been baptized (Mosiah 18:16). From these small beginnings of his own, Abinadi's convert eventually returned with his people to the land of Zarahemla, where King Mosiah asked Alma to speak to all his people and to "establish churches throughout all the land of Zarahemla" (Mosiah 25:14, 19). Alma the Elder also became a trusted friend of King Mosiah, who later conferred the plates of brass and other records to Alma's son, Alma (see Mosiah 28:20).[4] For all of us who relish the Book of Alma, it was a fateful decision.

Through his faith and prayers, Alma the Elder also helped bring about the conversion not only of his own prodigal son, but of King Mosiah's prodigal sons as well (see Mosiah 27:14, 18, 32). Thus, Abinadi's one known convert, Alma the Elder, not only brought hundreds of souls into the Church and taught thousands, but his prayers helped bring about the conversion of those who would be responsible for bringing the gospel to thousands of Lamanites and Nephites. Moreover, from the one man who hearkened to Abinadi's words descended a line of record keepers whose abridged writings account for just over fifty percent of the Book of Mormon (Alma through 4 Nephi as well as parts of Mosiah). Like Lehi, Nephi, and Jacob, Abinadi may not have taught many believers in mortality, but the impact of his earthly labors is truly eternal.

THEREFORE, WHAT?

Often we strive to emulate Church leaders in our lives. We should. But the vast majority of righteous Church members are destined to be Primary teachers and home teachers, ward clerks and compassionate service leaders, not General Authorities or members of the Relief Society General Board. For those of us who spend most of our lives serving in our wards and in our families, if we are not careful, we may somehow forget just how important labors performed out of the limelight can be. President Gordon B. Hinckley is quick to remind us that it is how we serve God that matters, not where:

> I wish to remind you that we are all in this together. It is not a matter of the General Authorities on one hand and the membership of the Church on the other. We are all working as one in a great cause. We are all members of the Church of Jesus Christ.
>
> Within your sphere of responsibility you have as serious an obligation as do I within my sphere of responsibility. Each of us should

be determined to build the kingdom of God on the earth and to further the work of righteousness.[5]

Through their examples, Book of Mormon prophets such as Lehi, Nephi, Jacob, and Abinadi powerfully testify of the truthfulness of President Hinckley's words. In striving simply to lead his family, Lehi received one of the most powerful visions recorded in scripture and taught one of the most illuminating sermons we have on the Fall, opposition, and agency (see 2 Nephi 2). Nephi's courage and faith were witnessed only by his family in his day, but they have inspired millions in ours. His brother's sermons were given to congregations probably no larger than most wards, yet Jacob's words have pro-foundly influenced the thinking of countless followers of Christ millennia after they were written.

Finally, Abinadi reminds us how we should approach that Primary class or deacons quorum that through some demographic fluke has just one member. Instead of wondering whether our talents are being underutilized, when we follow Abinadi's example we will pour our-selves into preparing lessons that will help change that one person's life. In fact, we will remember that when we help those we serve make lasting changes in their lives, the ripple effect of those changes and our labors will last for generations to come. Elder Henry B. Eyring reminds us how our efforts can touch people far beyond those in our classes and immediate families: "Your call has eternal consequences for others and for you. In the world to come, thousands may call your name blessed, even more than the people you serve here. They will be the ancestors and the descendants of those who chose eternal life because of something you said or did, or even what you were."[6]

Of course, the ultimate application of this principle is the teaching we do in our homes as parents. This is especially true for mothers,[7] many of whom have sacrificed the opportunity to pursue higher profile careers and the acclaim of the world in order to concentrate their efforts on teaching those few spirits the Lord has entrusted to them. Elder M. Russell Ballard provides comforting perspective to all who have sacrificed the opportunity to play in more glamorous venues before bigger crowds in order to teach a few choice sons or daughters of God:

> Sadly, in today's world, a person's importance is often judged by the size of the audience before which he or she performs. That is how media and sports programs are rated, how corporate prominence is sometimes determined, and often how governmental rank is obtained. That may be why roles such as father, mother, and missionary seldom receive standing ovations. Fathers, mothers, and missionaries "play" before very small audiences. Yet, in the eyes of the Lord, there may be only *one size* of audience that is of lasting importance—and that is just *one,* each one, you and me, and each *one* of the children of God. The irony of the Atonement is that it is infinite and eternal, yet it is applied individually, one person at a time.[8]

Thus, whether we labor as fathers or mothers or Scoutmasters for a few or stake presidents for the many, when we magnify our callings, the Lord will magnify our earthly efforts with eternal consequences.

THE GIFT OF A CALLING

Mormon and others teach us how to magnify our callings rather than be burdened by them.

If one could choose a time in the Book of Mormon during which to live, the unraveling period in Mormon and Moroni's day would likely not be anywhere near the top of the list. Likewise, of all the prophetic shifts of duty to be assigned, Mormon's watch would seem to be one of the least desirable. Mormon preached and fought in vain for over half a century as he watched his people spiritually and physically self-destruct. Perhaps no verse better describes his efforts and his heartache than Mormon 3:12:

> Behold, I had led them, notwithstanding their wickedness I had led them many times to battle, and had loved them, according to the love of God which was in me, with all my heart; and my soul had been poured out in prayer unto my God all the day long for them; nevertheless, it was without faith, because of the hardness of their hearts.

Despite Mormon's spiritually heroic efforts, his people simply would not repent, and he was ultimately forced to witness their nearly entire destruction.

Against this backdrop, then, an almost off-handed phrase in one of Mormon's epistles to his son, Moroni, is especially meaningful: "And now I, Mormon, speak unto you, my beloved brethren; and it is by the grace of God the Father, and our Lord Jesus Christ, and his holy will, because of *the gift of his calling unto me,* that I am permitted to speak unto you at this time" (Moroni 7:2; emphasis added). Under incomparably more favorable circumstances, many a bishop (I plead guilty), Primary president, Scoutmaster, or missionary has bemoaned his or her misfortune in having received a calling that seems overwhelming. Yet under some of the worst conditions ever documented, Mormon, the prophet destined to preside over the complete disintegration of Nephite civilization, speaks of the "*gift* of [the Lord's] calling unto me" (Moroni 7:2, emphasis added). Similarly, though Mormon must have known that Moroni's prospects for success in the ministry were even worse than his own, he offered his congratulations to his son when he learned of his call: "My beloved son, Moroni, I rejoice exceedingly that your Lord Jesus Christ hath been mindful of you, and hath called you to his ministry, and to his holy work" (Moroni 8:2).

Perhaps Mormon realized how blessed he was to be able to abridge a book of scripture that would centuries later play a pivotal role in the Restoration of the gospel and the conversion of millions of souls. He may have had some premonition or foreknowledge of how Moroni's mission would include not only burying the plates but mentoring the young prophet who would translate them. In referring to his calling as a "gift," Mormon was undoubtedly mindful of the sanctifying side effects of serving the Lord, even if no one else is saved by such efforts. Or maybe Mormon simply understood that anyone who has enjoyed the blessings of the Atonement should be ever eager and eternally grateful to serve the Redeemer, in any capacity. In any event, his example teaches us a powerful lesson about leadership in the Lord's kingdom: no matter how difficult and overwhelming our circumstances may seem, it is an honor and blessing to serve the Lord in any calling.

Mormon's attitude toward his calling provides just one of many important lessons on spiritual leadership in the Book of Mormon. In this chapter I summarize several (but certainly not all) of these insights into how to magnify our callings.

"RIDDING MY GARMENTS OF YOUR SINS"

Like Ezekiel (see Ezekiel 34) and Paul (see Acts 20:26–27), Jacob understood that if he failed to fulfill his duty to warn the people, he would be accountable for the sins they committed. Having been consecrated a priest and teacher together with his brother Joseph, Jacob noted:

> And we did magnify our office unto the Lord, taking upon us the responsibility, answering the sins of the people upon our own heads if we did not teach them the word of God with all diligence; wherefore, by laboring with our might their blood might not come upon our garments; otherwise their blood would come upon our garments, and we would not be found spotless at the last day (Jacob 1:19).

For Jacob, then, part of his motivation was his understanding that if he did not diligently teach the word of God to those in his charge, the sins of his people would be answered upon his head. Jacob spoke also of his duty in these terms:

> Now, my beloved brethren, I, Jacob, according to the responsibility which I am under to God, to magnify mine office with soberness, and that I might rid my garments of your sins, I come up into the temple this day that I might declare unto you the word of God (Jacob 2:2).

It is certainly true that if through our diligent efforts we "bring, save it be one soul unto [the Lord], how great shall be [our] joy with him in the kingdom of [the] Father" (D&C 18:15). But Jacob also understood the corollary to this concept: if we fail to do what we can to save those within our stewardship, we will bear some responsibility for their sins. President John Taylor taught the same principle: "If you do not magnify your callings, God will hold you responsible for those whom you might have saved had you done your duty."[1]

"THEY COULD NOT BEAR THAT ANY HUMAN SOUL SHOULD PERISH"

As important as a sense of duty was in motivating prophets like Jacob, an even more powerful motivating force behind their relentless labor was their love of God and His children—even when the conduct of those they served did not seem to warrant much love. In his seminal talk on reasons for serving, Elder Dallin H. Oaks taught that love of God and our fellow beings is the best basis for serving, not only because it is the purest but also because it is the most powerful motive: "If our service is to be most efficacious, it must be accomplished for the love of God and the love of his children."[2]

Would a sense of duty alone prompt the kind of consuming concern that Nephi had for his people? "I pray continually for [my people] by day, and mine eyes water my pillow by night, because of them; and I cry unto my God in faith, and I know that he will hear my cry" (2 Nephi 33:3). Jacob, too, was filled with that anxiety that comes from love for others: "I am desirous for the welfare of your souls. Yea, mine anxiety is great for you; and ye yourselves know that it ever has been" (2 Nephi 6:3).

Lehi prayed out of a similar concern, "even with all his heart, in behalf of his people" (1 Nephi 1:5). What makes Lehi's love especially noteworthy is the wickedness and intransigence of those whom he loved. The same people for whom he prayed so fervently were those who subsequently "did mock him because of the things which he testified of them" and became so angry with him that "they also sought his life, that they might take it away" (1 Nephi 1:19, 20). Mormon's people weren't much better, but he loved them no less than Lehi loved those whom he was called to serve: "Notwithstanding their wickedness I had led them many times to battle, and had loved them, *according to the love of God which was in me*, with all my heart; and my soul had been poured out in prayer unto my God all the day long for them" (Mormon 3:12; emphasis added). Presumably, Mormon was not speaking merely from book knowledge when he taught Moroni and us that "charity is the pure love of Christ, and it endureth forever; and whoso is found possessed of it at the last day, it shall be well with him" (Moroni 7:47). He further instructed: "Wherefore, my beloved brethren, pray unto the Father with all the energy of heart, that ye may be filled with this love" (Moroni 7:48). Mormon may well have prayed not only for his people, but also for the ability to love his people.

When we remember our own indebtedness to God, it is easier to love others who also stand in need of his mercy. The experiences of Enos and the sons of Ammon illustrate this principle. Enos prayed first for his own soul and finally heard a heavenly voice declaring, "Enos, thy sins are forgiven thee" (Enos 1:5). No sooner had he learned of his own forgiveness than Enos began pleading for others—first the Nephites and then the Lamanites, whose hostility must have made them challenging to love:

> Now, it came to pass that when I had heard these words I began to feel a desire for the welfare of my brethren, the Nephites; where-fore, I did pour out my whole soul unto God for them. . . .

And . . . I prayed unto him with many long strugglings for my
brethren, the Lamanites (Enos 1:9, 11).

In fact, Enos' newfound altruism ran so deep that he prayed not
only for his enemies, but for their descendants, pleading with God
that the Book of Mormon "might be brought forth at some future day
unto the Lamanites, that, perhaps, they might be brought unto
salvation" (Enos 1:13).

Ammon and his brethren had a similar inside-out epiphany.
Having experienced both overwhelming guilt for their sins and the
exquisite relief of forgiveness, they simply could not bear the thought
of anyone perishing in their sins: "Now they were desirous that salvation should be declared to every creature, for they could not bear
that any human soul should perish; yea, even the very thoughts that
any soul should endure endless torment did cause them to quake and
tremble" (Mosiah 28:3). Thus, motivated by love for distant cousins
they had never met, Ammon and his brethren labored for fourteen
years (see Alma 17:4) with faith, patience, and, ultimately, success
among the Lamanites—rather than take up arms against them and
destroy them, as other Nephites had advocated (see Alma 26:25).

Just as these sons of Mosiah shook at the prospect of others perishing, Nephi shuddered when he beheld the spiritual demise that
would befall his people centuries later: "I was overcome because of
my afflictions, for I considered that mine afflictions were great above
all, because of the destruction of my people, for I had beheld their
fall" (1 Nephi 15:5). That a man who had suffered so many afflictions
throughout his life would consider this knowledge of his descendants'
eventual destruction an affliction "great above all" speaks volumes
about his love for those whom he had never even met in mortality.

Fueled not only by duty but by the pure love of Christ, Book of

Mormon prophets served not just to rid their garments of the blood of their brethren, but to save those whom they served. Speaking of all those who are "ordained unto the high priesthood of the holy order of God," Alma wrote that they were "called by this holy calling . . . to teach his commandments unto the children of men, that they also might enter into his rest" (Alma 13:6). Mormon similarly saw his calling as a charge to save others: "Behold, I am a disciple of Jesus Christ, the Son of God. I have been called of him to declare his word among his people, that they might have everlasting life" (3 Nephi 5:13).

NO REST FOR THE RIGHTEOUS

Such love leads to untiring service. Even after passing the torch to his sons, who "did go forth among the people, to declare the word unto them[,] . . . Alma, also, himself, could not rest, and he also went forth" (Alma 43:1). When the Lord blessed Nephi, Helaman's son, with extraordinary powers, He lauded not once but twice Nephi's relentless service: "Blessed art thou, Nephi, for those things which thou has done; for I have beheld how thou hast *with unwearyingness* declared the word, which I have given unto thee, unto this people. . . . And now, because thou hast done this *with such unwearyingness,* behold, I will bless thee forever" (Helaman 10:4; emphasis added). Although Book of Mormon prophets must have heeded King Benjamin's advice for a man not to "run faster than he has strength" (Mosiah 4:27), they also clearly heeded the second part of King Benjamin's charge: "And again, it is expedient that he should be diligent, that thereby he might win the prize; therefore, all things must be done in order" (Mosiah 4:27).

SPEEDY DELIVERY

One of the ways in which true diligence can be measured is by how quickly we respond to the inconvenient promptings of the Spirit.

For example, the same Nephi whom the Lord commended for his dili-gence was told to "go and declare unto this people, that thus saith the Lord God, who is the Almighty: Except ye repent ye shall be smitten, even unto destruction" (Helaman 10:11). Just prior to receiving this charge from the Lord, Nephi had correctly foretold the murder of the chief judge and then been falsely accused and bound for the crime (see Helaman 9:19). When his innocence was finally established, Nephi was released and was on "his way towards his own house" (Helaman 10:2) when he received this revelation. Certainly, the Lord would not have begrudged this prophet a trip home to see his loved ones and refresh himself before fulfilling the Lord's charge to declare repentance to a hardened people. But Nephi would have none of that:

> And behold, now it came to pass that when the Lord had spoken these words unto Nephi, *he did stop and did not go unto his own house,* but did return unto the multitudes who were scattered about upon the face of the land, and began to declare unto them the word of the Lord which had been spoken unto him, concerning their destruc-tion if they did not repent (Helaman 10:12; emphasis added).

Alma's experience in Ammonihah was remarkably similar to Nephi's. On his first trip to that city, the people "withstood all his words, and reviled him, and spit upon him, and caused that he should be cast out of their city." Disappointed and distressed, he was heading for the next town when an angel instructed him to "return to the city of Ammonihah, and preach unto the people of the city; yea, preach unto them. Yea, say unto them, except they repent the Lord God will destroy them." Like Nephi, Alma did not hesitate to obey: "Now it came to pass that after Alma had received his message from the angel of the Lord he returned speedily to the land of Ammonihah" (Alma 8:13–18).

Upon entering the city, Alma was befriended and nourished by

Amulek, who had been forewarned of Alma's entrance by an angel (see Alma 10:7). Amulek must have been impressed by Alma's unflinching and instant response to the angel's command to return to preach to a people who had just spit upon him and literally run him out of town. By his own admission, Amulek's own response to earlier promptings of the Spirit was markedly less valiant: "Nevertheless, I did harden my heart, for I was called many times and I would not hear; therefore I knew concerning these things, yet I would not know; therefore I went on rebelling against God, in the wickedness of my heart, even until the fourth day of this seventh month, which is in the tenth year of the reign of the judges" (Alma 10:6).

Amulek's repentance and subsequent extraordinary sermons (see, for example, Alma 34) show us that there is hope for all of us who may initially be slow to hearken to the occasionally inconvenient promptings of the Spirit.

FOCUS, MY SON

Exactly why Amulek resisted the promptings of the Spirit, we do not know. He was, by his own account, "a man of no small reputation among all those who know me; yea, and behold, I have many kindreds and friends, and I have also acquired much riches by the hand of my industry" (Alma 10:4). Perhaps he feared the impact that a fundamental spiritual change would have on his social and economic status in a city where righteousness was so unfashionable. Indeed, when he finally did heed the call to serve, doing so required great sacrifice. After their difficult mission in Ammonihah was completed, Alma took his companion into his home due to Amulek's "having forsaken all his gold, and silver, and his precious things, which were in the land of Ammonihah, for the word of God, he being rejected by those who were once his friends and also by his father and his kindred" (Alma 15:16).

Such sacrifices are not always necessary in order to serve, but the willingness to make them is. Alma himself had given up much in secular terms when he perceived that he could no longer do justice to both his spiritual calling and his weighty judicial duties. He delivered up the judgment-seat to Nephihah so that he could wholly focus his efforts on matters of eternal consequence: "And this he did that he himself might go forth among his people . . . that he might preach the word of God unto them, to stir them up in remembrance of their duty, . . . seeing no way that he might reclaim them save it were in bearing down in pure testimony against them" (Alma 4:19).

Even more distracting than temporal pursuits can be carnal pursuits. Thus, Alma reminded his erstwhile prodigal son, Corianton, about the importance of remaining absolutely focused on his spiritual duties. He warned him against being "led away by any vain or foolish thing," with Exhibit A being "wicked harlots." Riches, too, were not to be the focus of Corianton's life: "For behold, you cannot carry them with you." Instead, Corianton's focus was to be the ministry (Alma 39:11–14, 16). Alma understood that unbridled passion as well as secular obsessions had diverted his son from fulfilling his priesthood duties. To fulfill his ministry, Corianton had to be able to exercise discipline and make the kinds of sacrifices his father and Amulek ultimately chose to make.

ANXIETY-INDUCED REVELATION

From the experiences of Alma the Younger, Nephi (Helaman's son), Alma the Elder, and Lehi an interesting pattern emerges: Frequently, their most personally rewarding revelations came as a result of their anguished prayers for their people. Both Alma the

Younger and Nephi were agonizing over people who had rejected God's word when they received the revelations discussed above. In Alma's case, "while he was journeying [toward the city of Aaron], being weighed down with sorrow, wading through much tribulation and anguish of soul, because of the wickedness of the people who were in the city of Ammonihah, . . . behold an angel of the Lord appeared unto him" (Alma 8:14). Before commanding Alma to return to the city of Ammonihah to give its inhabitants a final warning, the angel first gave Alma a reassuring revelation about his own standing with God—something about which he had not been praying at all. "Blessed art thou, Alma; therefore, lift up thy head and rejoice, for thou hast great cause to rejoice; for thou hast been faithful in keeping the commandments of God from the time which thou receivedst thy first message from him" (Alma 8:15). Nephi's revelation similarly came while "he was thus pondering—being much cast down because of the wickedness of the people of the Nephites, their secret works of darkness, and their murderings, and their plunderings, and all manner of iniquities—and it came to pass as he was thus pondering in his heart, behold, a voice came unto him" (Helaman 10:3) assuring him of how pleased the Lord was with him.

Alma the Elder also received a comforting revelation about his standing before God—as a result not of his prayers for himself, but of his prayers for others. The newly designated high priest was perplexed about how to handle a novel disciplinary matter, now that King Mosiah II declined to punish citizens charged with sins that apparently no longer violated civil law. Thus, Alma "went and inquired of the Lord what he should do concerning this matter, for he feared that he should do wrong in the sight of God" (Mosiah 26:13). In response, he received extraordinary eternal promises in a revelation that began on a personal note marvelously unrelated to the weighty priesthood matter about which he had been praying:

> Blessed art thou, Alma, and blessed are they who were baptized in the waters of Mormon. Thou art blessed because of thy exceeding faith in the words alone of my servant Abinadi. . . .
>
> And blessed art thou because thou hast established a church among this people; and they shall be established, and they shall be my people. . . .
>
> And because thou hast inquired of me concerning the transgressor, thou art blessed.
>
> Thou art my servant; and I covenant with thee that shalt have eternal life (Mosiah 26:15, 17, 19–20).

How ironic and instructive that Alma received the personal promise of eternal life in a revelation that came as a result of his prayer on behalf of other people and other matters. He prayed to know about the standing of transgressors in the eyes of the Lord, but in the process Alma received an assurance of his own standing with God.

The Book of Mormon actually begins with the prototype in this prophetic pattern. Father Lehi, anguishing over the unrepentant Israelites in Jerusalem, "prayed unto the Lord, yea, even with all his heart, in behalf of his people" (1 Nephi 1:5). The result was a truly glorious vision, which included a view of "God sitting upon his throne, surrounded with numberless concourses of angels" (1 Nephi 1:8). Once again, a prophet praying out of concern for his people had received a revelation that was personally edifying, to say the least: "For his soul did rejoice, and his whole heart was filled, because of the things which he had seen, yea, which the Lord had shown unto him" (1 Nephi 1:15).

Praying for others is certainly not the only way to receive revelation, but the experience of these prophets reveals a wonderful perk of magnifying our callings: we find some of our greatest personal blessings, including revelations and reassuring promptings, when we lose ourselves in the service of others.

THE TRUTH HURTS

Often the messages these prophets were called to deliver were unpopular and potentially offensive. Yet Book of Mormon prophets boldly shared these warnings. The Lord commended Nephi's son, Helaman, not only for his unwearyingness, but because he had shared God's word without regard to his own safety: "And thou hast not feared them, and hast not sought thine own life, but hast sought my will, and to keep my commandments" (Helaman 10:4). One of Helaman's contemporaries, Samuel, the Lamanite prophet, explained both why some people are disinclined to listen to true prophets and, implicitly, why we may be tempted to dilute God's message when sharing it, especially with tough crowds:

> If a prophet come among you and declareth unto you the word of the Lord, which testifieth of your sins and iniquities, ye are angry with him . . . because he testifieth that your deeds are evil.
>
> But behold, if a man shall come among you and shall say: Do this, and there is no iniquity; . . . and do whatsoever your heart desireth—and if a man shall come among you and say this, ye will receive him, and say that he is a prophet.
>
> Yea, ye will lift him up, and ye will give unto him of your substance; ye will give unto him of your gold, and of your silver, and ye will clothe him with your costly apparel; and because he speaketh flattering words unto you, and he saith that all is well, then ye will not find fault with him (Helaman 13:26–28).

For most members of the Church, there is little temptation in our callings to swing to the flattering extreme, telling people outright lies so that they will praise and even pay us. Yet these same forces may be at play in subtler ways: We might be tempted to rely heavily on entertaining stories when teaching youth rather than immersing them in the scriptures because it makes us a more popular teacher or speaker; we might be tempted to skip a First Presidency message that is relevant but, we fear, potentially offensive to a family we home teach; we might be tempted not to share the gospel with our friends because we fear they will be offended or will view us as pushy or weird. Samuel and his prophetic peers teach us by precept and by doctrine that true shepherds deliver God's message without diluting it because they fear God more than they fear their listeners.

More recently, Elder Dallin H. Oaks has reminded us that we should not look for entertaining or even enjoyable counsel from our leaders, but wise counsel—which may or may not be pleasant to hear. Elder Oaks shared a conversation he had with a fellow Apostle following a general conference:

> My friend said someone told him, "I surely enjoyed your talk." We agreed that this is not the kind of comment we like to receive. As my friend said, "I didn't give that talk to be *enjoyed*. What does he think I am, some kind of entertainer?" Another member of our quorum joined the conversation by saying, "That reminds me of the story of a good minister. When a parishioner said, 'I surely enjoyed your sermon today,' the minister replied, 'In that case, you didn't understand it.'"
>
> You may remember that this April conference I spoke on pornography. No one told me they "enjoyed" that talk—not one! In fact, there was nothing enjoyable in it even for me.
>
> I speak of these recent conversations to teach the principle that a message given by a General Authority at a general conference—a message prepared under the influence of the Spirit to further the work of the Lord—is not given to be enjoyed. It is given to inspire, to

edify, to challenge, or to correct. It is given to be heard under the influence of the Spirit of the Lord, with the intended result that the listener learns from the talk and from the Spirit what he or she should *do* about it.[3]

Similarly, when we discharge our duties in our callings and follow the promptings of the Spirit in our lives, we may occasionally say things that people *need* to hear, even though they won't necessarily *want* to hear them.

Of course, tough talk such as Jacob's is not always or even usually called for. Hence, Alma urged Shiblon to use "boldness, but not overbearance" (Alma 38:12). One danger in using prophets as a leadership model is that in their unique positions, they are called upon to say and do some things (for example, warn people to repent lest their city be destroyed) that most of us will never be asked to do. So before speaking too sharply, wise stewards emulate Jacob's example in seeking to know what God would have us say to those in our charge:

> But, notwithstanding the greatness of the task, I must do according to the strict commands of God, and tell you concerning your wickedness and abominations.
>
> I must tell you the truth according to the plainness of the word of God. For behold, as I inquired of the Lord, thus came the word unto me, saying: Jacob, get thou up into the temple on the morrow, and declare the word which I shall give thee unto this people (Jacob 2:10–11).

Jacob had the confidence to speak so bluntly because he was not simply getting his frustrations off his chest. Instead, he had first obtained his errand from the Lord. We are more likely to receive such guidance about our assignments when we heed Nephi's advice to engage in pre-performance prayer: "Ye must not perform any thing unto the Lord save in the first place ye shall pray unto the Father in the name of Christ" (2 Nephi 32:9).

Mormon followed this advice before writing his fiery epistle to Moroni, in which he denounced in no uncertain terms the doctrine of infant baptism: "And now, my son, I desire that ye should labor diligently, that this gross error should be removed from among you; for, for this intent I have written this epistle. For immediately after I had learned these things of you *I inquired of the Lord* concerning the matter. And the word of the Lord came to me by the power of the Holy Ghost" (Moroni 8:6–7; emphasis added).

THEREFORE, WHAT?

Reading about how Book of Mormon prophets and patriarchs magnified their callings inspires me to be less whiny, less lazy, and more loving. I realize that my worst day with the teachers quorum pales in comparison to the rejection encountered by Lehi, Mormon, and Moroni—all of whom managed to do a far better job of loving their people than I do. Moreover, they remind me that if I want to truly magnify my callings, I may occasionally have to unload some of my secular pursuits and momentary comforts. When inspired, I may even have to sacrifice the short-term approval of those I serve if I wish to earn their long-term gratitude, or at least the approval of the Lord.

For me, these and other leadership lessons from the Book of Mormon were brought home one Christmas season when I was feeling a bit fatigued. To coordinate the welfare needs of those traveling through our stake or otherwise transient, the stake president designated one bishop in the stake as the "transient bishop," responsible for fielding all matters involving such individuals. It seemed as though the transient bishop's name was literally written in the phone booth of some low-cost motels in the area, because we frequently received calls from a wide variety of people in need, including many who were not members of the Church but pretended to be. With two weeks left in December, I confess that I found myself looking forward to passing this responsibility to another bishop. I practically held my breath, hoping to glide through the last two weeks of the year without another of these telephone calls.

It was not to be. On December 23, I received a phone call from a woman in need. Having been promised employment, she had moved to our area from Hawaii with her two teenage daughters. Unfortunately, the promised job had fallen through, and she was left with no funds, sleeping on the floor of her cousin's apartment. A cousin in Nevada promised to put her up and help her find a job if she could somehow find transportation.

After seeking the guidance of the Spirit, calling the Church's membership hotline to verify her membership, and attempting to call her previous bishop and her cousin in Nevada, I made arrangements to purchase one-way bus tickets for this woman and her daughters. She would leave the morning after next for Nevada. When I called to let her know that one of my counselors would deliver the tickets to her the next morning, she was genuinely grateful. I breathed a sigh of relief and assumed my job was done.

It was not. That evening as I prayed, reviewing the events of the day with Heavenly Father, he sweetly chastised me. I had been so intent on resolving the welfare matter as quickly as possible that I had scarcely noticed the calendar. It was as if Heavenly Father whispered to me, "So you're just going to put her on a bus on Christmas morning and call it good? Is that the best you can do?"

The next morning I called back, almost obligatorily, and asked if this sister and her daughters would like to spend Christmas Eve with my family. Still not nearly as Christ-like as I should have been, I may have even secretly hoped that she would decline my offer and let me off the hook. Instead, she was genuinely delighted by the prospect and accepted the invitation on behalf of herself and one daughter. (The other chose to spend Christmas Eve with her cousins.)

My heart began to change that evening when we picked up this sister and her daughter, and I saw the blankets on the floor where she had been sleeping. They didn't have much, but they were wearing the best clothes they had brought with them. They enthusiastically joined in all our activities for the evening along with our other three guests—from enacting the nativity story to singing Christmas carols while I played the accordion. When we invited everyone to share their feelings about the Savior, the daughter spoke tenderly about how strongly she had felt the Spirit in our home as we sang and how grateful she was to be there. And when we asked everyone to share their favorite Christmas memory, the mother said with emotion and without hesitation, "This one."

It is now my favorite Christmas memory as well. It helped me realize that what seemed a tiresome duty two days earlier was, in fact, a sweet gift—the gift of having a calling that helped me finally lose myself and find the joy that comes with serving others.

THE PAHORAN PRINCIPLE

—◦—

From Pahoran's generous response in a stressful situation,
we learn the importance of being slow to take offense, quick to forgive,
and ready to glean wisdom.

Perhaps no reason is more frequently cited for falling out of activity in the Church than the actions of Church leaders or members that are perceived (justifiably or not) as offensive. Indeed, even among active members, sparks sometimes fly as the rough edges of our personalities collide. As Elder Neal A. Maxwell has written, "In a perfect church filled with imperfect people, there are bound to be some miscommunications at times."[1] Mormon may well have had such challenges in mind when he included a fascinating exchange between the Nephite chief captain, Moroni, and the chief governor, Pahoran, at the end of the book of Alma.[2] Their correspondence provides valuable insights into how we can better deal with our fellow laborers in the kingdom, even in the most stressful of circumstances.

I was once approached by a sister upset with a decision another ward member had made in his calling. When I suggested that she might want to review Pahoran's story, she declared, "This is different—I'm right!"

What is so inspiring and illuminating about Pahoran's conduct is that he *was* right. Although probably not without fault himself, Pahoran had far more cause to take offense than most of us do when some remark or decision fills us with righteous indignation. Indeed, the Savior's command to forgive others' trespasses (see, for example, Mosiah 26:31) applies precisely when we have been wronged. Pahoran's measured response provides us all with a much needed example of how to, in the words of Elder Maxwell, "absorb unjust criticism."[3]

THE SITUATION

The stage for the exchange between Moroni and Pahoran is set by Helaman's moving and distressing epistle to Moroni, found in Alma 56–58. After recounting the miraculous victories of his stripling warriors, Helaman warns Moroni that "our armies are small to maintain so great a number of cities and so great possessions" (Alma 58:32). Full of faith, Helaman trusted that "God will deliver us, notwithstanding the weakness of our armies" (Alma 58:37). Still, Helaman cannot help but wonder "the cause that the government does not grant us more strength" (Alma 58:34). Perhaps the government in Zarahemla does not send the needed reinforcements, ventures Helaman, because "there is some faction in the government" (Alma 58:36).

This news undoubtedly filled Moroni with a mixture of compassion for Helaman's men and frustration with the government in Zarahemla. He promptly sends an epistle to Pahoran requesting reinforcements and supplies (see Alma 59:3). For reasons we are not told, Pahoran does not respond.

Helaman's suspicions about civil strife in Zarahemla proved to be well founded. Infatuated with the power of a monarchy, king-men had once again rebelled against the chief judge. However, this time the monarchists had succeeded in installing a king in Zarahemla and driving out Pahoran's legitimate government. Pahoran was leading his government in exile from the land of Gideon, where he was rallying opposition to the new king and mulling over whether to mount an attack against him (see Alma 61:3–6, 19).

Whether Pahoran even received Helaman's epistle and Moroni's first epistle during this time of turmoil is unclear. If he did receive them, we can only speculate as to why he did not respond.[4] He may have been negligent in failing to respond, but we eventually learn Pahoran was still clearly committed to the cause of freedom and was preoccupied by civil war.

MORONI'S VERBAL OFFENSIVE

Deeply concerned for his men's safety and his country's future, Moroni holds nothing back in his second letter to Pahoran. Early on, Moroni announces that he is writing to Pahoran "by the way of condemnation" (Alma 60:2). Initially, Moroni's principal charge against Pahoran is neglect. Moroni declares that thousands of deaths could have been prevented—if only Pahoran had sent the requested reinforcements (see Alma 60:5). Indeed, writes Moroni, "ye have neglected them insomuch that the blood of thousands shall come upon your heads for vengeance" (Alma 60:10).

Moroni also decries Pahoran's "thoughtless stupor" toward his troops on the front line (Alma 60:7). Midway through his epistle, Moroni openly wonders whether Pahoran has joined the ranks of the royal rebels (see Alma 60:18). Or maybe the security and comfort of the judgment-seat have made Pahoran indifferent to the hardships of the men in the field (see Alma 60:19). Whatever the cause for the government's neglect, this much is clear to Moroni: things on the domestic front must be cleansed—even if doing so requires the use of force (see Alma 60:23–27). Moroni then applies this principle to Pahoran, with chilling and increasing specificity. "Except ye repent . . . and begin to be up and doing" and promptly send reinforcements, Moroni threatens, "it will be expedient that we contend no more with the Lamanites until we have first cleansed our inward vessel, yea, even the great head of our government" (Alma 60:24).

Lest his point be lost on Pahoran, Moroni makes it even more sharply. Unless Pahoran shows "the true spirit of freedom," Moroni will rally the people against the usurpers of power until they "shall become extinct" (Alma 60:25–27). Indeed, unless Pahoran grants the needed assistance, vows Moroni, "I come unto you . . . and smite you with the sword" (Alma 60:30). Moroni suspects a lust for power has perverted Pahoran from the right way: "Your iniquity is for the cause of your love of glory and the vain things of the world" (Alma 60:32). He began his epistle alleging mostly negligence, but he seems to have gotten on an emotional roll while writing it. By the conclusion, Moroni flatly charges Pahoran: "Ye know that ye do transgress the laws of God, and ye do know that ye do trample them under your feet" (Alma 60:33).

PAHORAN'S PATIENCE

Pahoran may well have been remiss in failing to keep his chief general apprised of the trouble in the Nephite capital. It may also have been possible for him to do more to keep Moroni's troops supplied and reinforced. However, Moroni clearly missed the mark in assuming Pahoran had cavalierly caused the deaths of Nephite soldiers or trampled the laws of God under his feet. In 1942, Elder Harold B. Lee described Moroni as "mistakenly reproving Pahoran 'for sitting upon his throne in a state of thoughtless stupor.'"[5] Similarly, Elder Neal A. Maxwell has referred to Moroni's criticism of Pahoran as "unjust"[6] and his rhetoric as "harsh."[7] Such unfair accusations and personal death threats by a subordinate would have rankled virtually any chief executive, to say the very least.

Yet if Moroni's words outraged Pahoran, there is no hint of such anger or even frustration in his reply. After informing his chief captain of the actual circumstances in Zarahemla, Pahoran refers only briefly and charitably to Moroni's indictments: "And now, in your epistle you have censured me, but it mattereth not; I am not angry, but do rejoice in the greatness of your heart" (Alma 61:9). We can only imagine how terrible Moroni must have felt upon learning how wrong he had been—and how relieved he must have been to know that Pahoran would not hold such mistakes against him.

In dismissing Moroni's mistake without any kind of reprimand, Pahoran must have known and focused on Moroni's remarkable track record as well as the intent of his heart. While Moroni incorrectly surmised that Pahoran was seeking for power, Pahoran undoubtedly knew that Moroni spoke the truth when he claimed that he himself sought "not for power, but to pull it down" (Alma 60:36). By focusing on "the greatness of [Moroni's] heart," Pahoran managed to respond with remarkable restraint and perspective.

GLEANING WISDOM

Pahoran's response attests that his forgiveness of Moroni's mistake was not merely cosmetic. Pahoran actually thanks Moroni for shedding light on a strategic and moral issue that had been vexing him: whether to attack the self-anointed king in Zarahemla. "And now, Moroni, I do joy in receiving your epistle, for I was somewhat worried concerning what we should do, whether it should be just in us to go against our brethren. But ye have said, except they repent the Lord hath commanded you that ye should go against them" (Alma 61:19–20).

In the very advice Pahoran quotes from Moroni, Moroni had actually stated that unless *Pahoran* repented, Moroni would come against him. Far less offensive comments have driven lasting wedges between leaders and friends, or at least caused them to tune out the remaining counsel from the offending source. But Pahoran simply compensated for Moroni's lack of information and applied Moroni's counsel as Moroni would have, had he known all the facts. Thus, Pahoran refused to let Moroni's factual mistakes distract him from appreciating Moroni's inspired doctrinal and strategic advice.

In light of Moroni's counsel, Pahoran instructed Moroni to leave most of his men in the charge of Lehi and Teancum, bringing with him a small group of men and rallying others to the cause as he marched home. Together, Pahoran and Moroni would then retake Zarahemla and cleanse the inner vessel. In the meantime, Pahoran would send what provisions he could to bolster Moroni's troops (see Alma 61:15–18). Relieved to learn that Pahoran was not a traitor, Moroni promptly obeyed Pahoran's commands (see Alma 62:1). Throughout Alma 62, we then read of Moroni and Pahoran's united efforts as they overthrew the king-men, "restored peace to the land of Zarahemla," and marched on to retake the city of Nephihah (see Alma 62:6–7, 11, 14, 26). Surely, Pahoran's generous response facilitated such conquering cooperation.

THEREFORE, WHAT?

A friend who read a draft of this chapter raised an intriguing possibility: What if the response we read from Pahoran in Alma 62 weren't his first draft? Whether this response was his first draft or his fourth, he has my admiration either way.

Personally, I certainly have not yet progressed to the point where I could take a letter like Moroni's in stride; far lesser accusations have caused me to lose sleep. But as I strive to reach that point of mellow steadiness, I am learning to sit on my fiery first draft of a response for at least a day. When I've waited, I've rarely sent that first response—and I've never regretted waiting.

My time as bishop also makes me very slow to criticize any Church leader, however imperfect, who puts in tireless unseen hours of service. Pahoran undoubtedly had Moroni's tireless efforts on behalf of his country in mind when writing his response. When we remember how hard our fellow laborers are trying, it makes it easier to judge them in their callings as we'd like to be judged in ours. I find I can ignore even the worst call an official makes in a Church basketball game if I simply remember that he's an amateur voluntarily staying until 10:00 at night so that men or boys can play ball.

If I'm feeling especially Christ-like, I even strive to follow Pahoran's example and glean wisdom in a tirade from an angry ward member or from a colleague. Like Moroni, they may not be right about everything, but if I humble myself enough, I discover they are usually right about something. And if I am wise, I manage to muster even more deference for the conduct of those whom the Lord has called to preside over me.[8] My goal is to reach the point, like Pahoran, where, cloaked in charity, I "grudge not" (James 5:9) and am not easily provoked (see Moroni 7:45).

Like Pahoran, men and women of Christ realize their fellow laborers in the kingdom are usually doing their best under sometimes difficult circumstances. Thus, they judge others as mercifully in fulfilling their callings as they wish to be judged in their own. In doing so, they avoid the counterproductive bitterness that stems from a preoccupation with proving they are right. Finally, as with Pahoran, their ability to forgive and forge ahead blesses not only their own lives but also the lives of their fellow leaders and those whom they serve.

LESSONS FOR
THE CONFLICT

SATAN'S SLIPPERY SLOPES

The adversary carefully customizes his appeals to lure us away from the strait and narrow path one step at a time.

The devil is a dirty fighter," Elder M. Russell Ballard has warned, "and we must be aware of his tactics."[1] Not surprisingly, then, Mormon chooses to give a fair number of column inches, as it were, to the arguments of anti-Christs and tactics of the adversary. Once again, Mormon's editorial choice was dictated by his intended audience. As President Ezra Taft Benson noted, "The type of apostates in the Book of Mormon are similar to the type we have today. God, with his infinite foreknowledge, so molded the Book of Mormon that we might see the error and know how to combat false educational, political, religious, and philosophical concepts of our time."[2]

As we scrutinize both the teachings of the Book of Mormon's anti-Christs and the arguments of the adversary, two important, overarching patterns emerge.

First, the adversary is nimble, customizing temptations and arguments to play to our weaknesses. Second, he works incrementally, beginning with subtle deviations from the path of righteousness and eventually working his way up to dramatic detours. Sherem, Nehor, the Zoramites, and Korihor give us living examples of how the adversary is both flexible and progressive in his attempts with each new pitch to lead us farther away from the iron rod.

MANY LIES WILL DO

A criminal defense lawyer can sometimes win a case by leading jurors to suspect that any number of people—indeed, anyone but the accused—committed the crime in question. Similarly, the adversary succeeds when we choose any path but the strait and narrow path that leads to life. These alternate routes may lead in opposite directions from each other, but they fulfill Satan's purpose as long as they lead us away from God.

Nephi prophesied about some of the competing arguments the adversary would advance in our day, sometimes through unwitting spokesmen. Some religious leaders, Nephi notes, will argue that "there is no God today, for the Lord and the Redeemer hath done his work, and he hath given his power unto men" (2 Nephi 28:5).

Yet many others will say, more agnostically, "Eat, drink, and be merry, for tomorrow we die; and it shall be well with us" (2 Nephi 28:7). Still others would sound a slightly more cautious variation on the theme of seizing the day: "Eat, drink, and be merry; nevertheless, fear God—he will justify in committing a little sin; . . . for tomorrow we die; and if it so be that we are guilty, God will beat us with a few stripes, and at last we shall be saved in the kingdom of God" (2 Nephi 28:8).

Nephi foresaw one especially striking pair of contradictory arguments in our day. On the one hand, Satan will try to seduce some of us into inaction by praising our prosperity, creating a false sense of spiritual well-being: "And others will he pacify, and lull them away into carnal security, that they will say: All is well in Zion; yea, Zion prospereth, all is well—and thus the devil cheateth their souls, and leadeth them away carefully down to hell" (2 Nephi 28:21). To others who may be less religiously inclined, Lucifer paints the very idea of hell and a devil as preposterous: "And behold, others he flattereth away, and telleth them there is no hell; and he saith unto them: I am no devil, for there is none—and thus he whispereth in their ears, until he grasps them with his awful chains, from whence there is no deliverance" (2 Nephi 28:22).

Which is it? Are things going so well in Zion that there's no need to improve? Or is there no need to improve because there is no hell and no devil? These are two very different arguments, but the result is the same if we buy into either fallacy: we will not improve. Just as a good quarterback takes advantage of what the defense gives him, Satan seizes on our weaknesses and hits us where we are most vulnerable.

None of these arguments is intended to appeal to everyone. Instead, while he suggests to some that they eat, drink, and be merry, "*others* will he pacify" and yet "*others* he flattereth away" (2 Nephi 28:21–22; emphasis added). Clearly, the adversary crafts different arguments for different groups of people. If we are naturally lazy, he may lobby us to spend more time watching TV; if we are naturally ambitious, he pushes us to spend more time at the office. If we are slow to recognize our mistakes (or have become numb to the Spirit), he will tell us we've done nothing wrong and have no need to repent. But if we begin to experience sorrow that leads to repentance (see Mormon 2:13), he may try to convince us our sin is so great that repentance isn't possible. He can prey on lack of self-esteem as well as pride, self-righteousness as well as atheism, the theology of grace as well as an exclusive emphasis on works. In sum, Satan's spinmasters are nothing if not nimble in tailoring their campaign speeches to different constituencies.

EASY DOES IT—A CASE STUDY

From the devil's perspective, any road that leads away from the strait and narrow path is good, but the farther we stray from the path of righteousness, the better. As we wander farther afield, our return becomes both more difficult and less likely. Thus, the adversary is not content to leave us alone simply because we have slipped onto a path that deviates slightly from the one charted by God. Instead, he will try to gently coax us farther and farther from the path we once walked or should be walking—one step at a time: "He leadeth them by the neck with a flaxen cord, until he bindeth them with his strong cords forever" (2 Nephi 26:22). As President James E. Faust put it, "We all have an inner braking system that will stop us before we follow Satan too far down the wrong road. . . . But once we have succumbed, the braking system begins to leak brake fluid and our stopping mechanism becomes weak and ineffective."[3]

In fact, when we reject light and knowledge, we contribute to our own incremental demise. "For behold, thus saith the Lord God: . . . from them that shall say, We have enough, from them shall be taken away even that which they have" (2 Nephi 28:30). Just as obedience leads to greater light and knowledge (see Alma 12:10), disobedience places us on Satan's slippery slope: "And they that will harden their hearts, to them is given the lesser portion of the word until they know nothing concerning his mysteries; and then they are taken captive by the devil, and led by his will down to destruction. Now this is what is meant by the chains of hell" (Alma 12:11).

Sherem, Nehor, the Zoramites, and Korihor give us a revealing glimpse into how Satan's arguments evolve along his slippery slope away from the strait and narrow path. Each one presents a fundamentally different worldview, each inconsistent with the others, but the adversary who inspired the arguments of these anti-Christs must have been pleased with each approach.

Sherem. Chronologically and conceptually, we begin with Sherem, whose arguments may have represented the smallest (though still significant) deviation from the strait and narrow path. Like later anti-Christs, Sherem "preached many things which were flattering unto the people" (Jacob 7:2). Sherem cloaked himself in righteousness and the law of Moses (see Jacob 7:7), actively seeking out the prophet, Jacob, to correct him (see Jacob 7:3). When he finally gained the opportunity to speak directly to the aging prophet, Sherem wasted no time in accusing Jacob of committing blasphemy:

> And ye have led away much of this people that they pervert the right way of God, and keep not the law of Moses which is the right way; and convert the law of Moses into the worship of a being which ye say shall come many hundred years hence. And now behold, I, Sherem, declare unto you that this is blasphemy; for no man knoweth of such things; for he cannot tell of things to come[4] (Jacob 7:7).

Paradoxically, it was, of course, Sherem who was perverting the law of Moses from a schoolmaster whose "whole meaning . . . point[s] to that great and last sacrifice" of Christ (Alma 34:14; see also Galatians 3:24) into an abstract set of rules and rituals with no connection to the Messiah who gave them. Thus, even though he purported to defend the law God gave to Moses, Sherem's arguments were appealing enough to the adversary that Sherem was given "much power of speech, according to the power of the devil" (Jacob 7:4). Satan has always been willing to lace his arguments with truth, as long as the end result is to lead people away from God.

Nehor. Centuries later, during the reign of Alma the Younger, Nehor came onto the scene with an approach that foreshadowed modern-day self-help gurus. Like Sherem, Nehor preached "that which he termed to be the word of God" (Alma 1:3). But while Sherem sounded more like the scribes of Christ's day—who also could not see the forest of the Messiah through the trees of the law of Moses—Nehor's approach was more populist than Pharasaic. He taught a soothing doctrine designed to appeal to those with "itching ears" (2 Timothy 4:3): "that all mankind should be saved at the last day, and that they need not fear nor tremble, but that they might lift up their heads and rejoice; for the Lord had created all men, and had also redeemed all men; and, in the end, all men should have eternal life" (Alma 1:4). The fallacy of such a doctrine, of course, is that it incorrectly asserts that salvation is guaranteed for all and that how we live, what we believe, and whether we repent are completely irrelevant, which ideas are of course blatantly false.

As Samuel the Lamanite observed shortly before the coming of Christ, "because [a false prophet] speaketh flattering words unto you, and he saith that all is well, then ye will not find fault with him" (Helaman 13:28). Not surprisingly, then, the masses liked what they heard from Nehor, and "many did believe on his words, even so many that they began to support him and give him money" (Alma 1:5). This may have been exactly what Nehor had in mind when he argued that "every priest and teacher ought to become popular; and they ought not to labor with their hands, but that they ought to be supported by the people" (Alma 1:3). Nehor had discovered something practiced by religious opportunists since the beginning: that preachers who tell people what they want to hear not only become popular but can get their listeners to support them financially.

The Lord has organized His church in such a way as to minimize the risk of such things. Saints are assigned to congregations based on where they live, eliminating any temptation for local leaders to compete for members. And since local leaders labor to support them-selves (see, for example, Alma 1:26; Mosiah 2:14), they have no finan-cial incentive to preach doctrines that merely please rather than save.

The Zoramites. The Zoramites were a group of apostate Nephites (see Alma 31:8) who had established their own religious beliefs and practices. Like Sherem, they did not accept the doctrine of a Messiah, declaring it to be a false notion stemming from "the foolish traditions of our brethren, which doth bind them down to a belief of Christ, which doth lead their hearts to wander far from . . . God" (Alma 31:17). And with an arrogance reminiscent of Nehor's, the Zoramites insisted they alone were destined for salvation, a smugness that made it easy for them to disdain all others. From a raised stand they called Rameumptom or "holy stand," they would pray, "[T]hou hast elected us that we shall be saved, whilst all around us are elected to be cast by thy wrath down to hell[,]" adding with almost comical self-righteousness, "for the which holiness, O God, we thank thee" (Alma 31:17).

The Zoramites' basis for believing God had singled them out for salvation is unclear, since they eschewed not only Christ but also the commandments under the law of Moses (see Alma 31:9). In any event, they were zealous in meeting weekly (see Alma 31:12) to repeat these messages to each other, after which they "returned to their homes, never speaking of their God again until they had assembled themselves together again to the holy stand" (Alma 31:23). Daily reminders of their religion may not have been necessary, in their view, since their beliefs apparently required no action on their part but a public declaration of their chosen state.

Korihor. The Book of Mormon's best-known anti-Christ, Korihor, also emerged during the pluralistic reign of Alma the Younger. While Nehor claimed to preach God's word, Korihor made no such pretense.

Like Sherem, Korihor summarily dismissed the ability of anyone to know of things that are to come: "Why do ye look for a Christ? For no man can know of anything which is to come" (Alma 30:13). But unlike Sherem, Korihor unabashedly dismissed everything "handed down by holy prophets" as "foolish traditions" (Alma 30:14). With that captivating command of language that Satan lends to his spokespeople in all genres, Korihor mocked those foolish enough to believe in the faith of their fathers: "[I]t is the effect of a frenzied mind; and this derangement of your minds comes because of the traditions of your fathers, which lead you away into a belief of things which are not so" (Alma 30:16).

Korihor also pitched a doctrine that may have been especially appealing to hard-working, ambitious, yet self-absorbed individuals. He taught that "every man fared in this life according to the management of the creature; therefore every man prospered according to his genius, and that every man conquered according to his strength" (Alma 30:17). Like so many of Satan's sound bites, Korihor's teaching on this point is a perversion of a true doctrine: "And inasmuch as ye shall keep my commandments, ye shall prosper" (1 Nephi 2:20). Korihor simply attributes prosperity to our own hard work and intelligence rather than our obedience, thus removing God from the equation.

Korihor also belittled those who feared their conduct would "offend some unknown being, who [the priests] say is God—a being who never has been seen or known, who never was nor ever will be" (Alma 30:28). Nor did Korihor believe people should keep commandments in hopes of some kind of eternal reward, declaring that "when a man [is] dead, that [is] the end thereof" (Alma 30:18). As for morality, Korihor brazenly taught, "whatsoever a man did was no crime" (Alma 30:17).[5] While Sherem and Nehor offered up misleading, diluted versions of God's word, Korihor moved several steps further away from the strait and narrow path by altogether dismissing the reality of sin and the afterlife and by denying even the existence of God.

THEREFORE, WHAT?

Personally, I prefer to focus on the temptations and tactics that don't much appeal to me; it makes me feel as though I'm doing well. I'd rather hear a talk denouncing murder than pride, since I'm doing a pretty good job so far in obeying the commandment not to kill. But when I remember that Satan is nimble, incremental, and shrewd, I realize I need to be aware of the tactics he's most likely to use against me. That helps me understand that I really do need to hear the talk on pride—and that I should even question whether he's chipping away at my respect for the sanctity of life by desensitizing me to violence in films.

When I consider the talented but evil men described in the Book of Mormon and how they were able persuade the people to set aside the truth, it makes me realize that I need to carefully screen the work of some of my favorite songwriters, actors, comedians, and other performers. They're certainly not anti-Christs, but the same singer who performs a beautiful and wholly appropriate love song on one track of a CD may inform me on another that it's better to "laugh with the sinners than cry with the saints, the sinners are much more fun."[6] One of the things I am prompted to do when reading these passages in the Book of Mormon is to become a more careful consumer of ideas.

That means I need to pay a bit more attention to lyrics, for starters. Our whole family was recently riding together in the car when I began singing along with what I thought was a wonderful rock song from the 80s. Actually, I was pretty much singing along with just one word in the chorus because that was all I really knew.

"What are you thinking?" my wife asked with a certain directness that has proved very helpful through the years.

"What?" I protested, thinking she was objecting to the quality of my voice. "I'm just singing along."

"Do you have any idea what this song is about?" she pressed.

"Yes, I do," I replied confidently. I then repeated the woman's name who was the subject of the chorus. At my wife's suggestion, I listened to the rest of the lyrics and was surprised to learn that the woman being celebrated in this song was a prostitute. It was a revealing moment. I am quite sure that on other occasions, I've sung along with more than one word of a tune whose message was fundamentally at odds with the gospel. Satan and his minions must chuckle when they manage to slip ideas past us in song or film—and even get us to repeat them—ideas or notions that we would never support if they were mere words, unvarnished with catchy music or flashy special effects.

SPIRITUAL COMBAT TRAINING

*The Book of Mormon chapters about war are rich with insights
for our own battles with the adversary.*

Like many readers, I have been tempted to skim through the war chapters of the Book of Mormon, figuring that if I ever became a general I would be sure to study those chapters more carefully. When we succumb to this temptation, however, we miss out on the many spiritually strategic insights these chapters contain—insights that are applicable far beyond the military arena. My suspicion is that these chapters were no more intended to be a purely military treatise than the Savior's parables were intended to be an instruction manual for farmers. More than merely showing us how to fight physical battles against mortal enemies, these chapters show us how to fight spiritual battles against an immortal foe. When we read these chapters looking for such insights—viewing Captain Moroni as a type of God's prophets and his enemies as symbols for the adversary and his minions—we discover the key to a slew of marvelously applicable insights from these often overlooked passages of the Book of Mormon.[1]

HATRED BLINDS

Given the horrors of war—especially in the days of hand-to-hand combat—rushing headlong into battle was probably not something most soldiers were willing to do without some compelling reason. For those fighting in defense of their families, their lands, their lives, and their freedom, powerful motivation was easy enough to find. But for leaders fighting offensive and unjust wars, motivating the troops to risk injury and death was surely more problematic.

Zerahemnah must have known this when he appointed the Zoramites and Amalekites to be chief captains and, in effect, propaganda ministers (see Alma 43:6). These leaders gathered support for an offensive and irrational war by stirring up hatred against the Nephites: "Now this he did that he might preserve their hatred towards the Nephites, that he might bring them into subjection to the accomplishment of his designs" (Alma 43:7). Zerahemnah understood well the blinding power of hatred; thus, "his designs were to stir up the Lamanites to anger against the Nephites" (Alma 43:8). Fueled by this manufactured hatred for their Nephite cousins, the Lamanites fought boldly—in circumstances where men not blinded by such anger could have seen the futility and injustice of their cause (see, for example, Alma 43:19–20).

In our day, Satan continues to harness the power of hatred not only in national and ethnic conflicts, but in personal conflicts as well. His minions strive to stir us up against each other—sometimes by spreading outright lies and sometimes by dwelling on unfortunate truths about the weaknesses of those whom he would have us hate. Whether our hatred is rooted in fact or fiction, the consuming result is the same: we can no longer see clearly. Thus, we may find ourselves charging into or prolonging battles that are as foolish, dangerous, and unnecessary as the Lamanites' attacks on the Nephites.

PRAYING ON THE JOB

Captain Moroni was engaged in what could be called a righteous secular or civic activity—protecting his nation. Yet "knowing the prophecies of Alma," he did not hesitate to send messengers to the prophet to seek divine direction (see Alma 43:23). Consequently, without the aid of satellite surveillance, Alma received accurate and invaluable intelligence about the enemy's location and intentions (see Alma 43:24). Later, Moroni made direct supplication to the Lord for assistance in "the cause of the Christians, [that] the freedom of the land might be favored" (Alma 46:16).

We may be quick to seek the Lord's help and guidance in magnifying our callings or other spiritual matters, but Moroni's example reminds us that we can seek divine direction and blessing in our righteous secular pursuits as well. I remember one experience as a young lawyer where I was struggling to find documentation on a group of cases on a particular topic. My challenge was much like trying to look up a business in the phone book, without knowing exactly under which heading the business was listed. Finally, in my frustration I prayed, and the word *corporations* immediately came to my mind. I quickly flipped to the section of the legal treatise on corporations, and within seconds I located the exact line of cases I had been struggling to find.

My experience and Mormon's example remind me that whether providing for our families, obtaining education, or engaging in community affairs, our efforts will be more productive when we seek inspiration and aid from Heavenly Father.

REAL FAITH AND REAL SHIELDS

While Moroni was quick to seek the Lord's blessing and guidance, he did not naively assume that the Lord would take care of his problems without further effort on his part. Thus, in addition to the miraculous surveillance provided through Alma, Moroni learned "by his spies which course the Lamanites were to take" (Alma 43:30). Similarly, even though his men were engaged in a just cause worthy of divine protection, Moroni furnished them with all the physical protection he could. He "prepared his people with breastplates and with arm-shields, yea, and also shields to defend their heads, and also they were dressed with thick clothing" (Alma 43:19).

Occasionally some Latter-day Saints with extraordinary faith may fear that taking prudent actions of their own somehow demonstrates a lack of faith. Alternatively, their trust in God may pacify them into thinking they do not need to be as diligent in accomplishing a task because "the Lord will provide." Captain Moroni provides us with a powerful reminder that it is more than acceptable to plead for God's help and then work hard ourselves toward accomplishing the same end. Indeed, Moroni exemplifies the familiar counsel to pray as if everything depended on the Lord and then to work as if everything depended on us. One suspects that a modern Moroni would no more forgo medicine, for example, than he would deny his men protective armor. Similarly, it is easy to imagine that Moroni would heartily approve of research conducted to quantify the effectiveness of various missionary approaches. Moroni clearly understood that the nobility of a cause justifies us in—rather than excuses us from—engaging in strategic and tactical thinking: "He thought it no sin that he should defend them by strategem" (Alma 43:30).

THE POWER OF ONE[2]

After they were rebuffed by Moroni in the battles described in Alma 43 and 44, the Lamanites might well have been content to live in peace, had it not been for the ambition of a single man—

Amalickiah. Having failed in his attempts to become the king of the Nephites by acclamation, he fled to the Lamanites and tried to rule the Nephites by annexation. Much of the bloodshed that occurs in the ensuing chapters can be laid squarely at the feet of Amalickiah (and, after his death, his brother, Ammaron). As Mormon observes, "we also see the great wickedness one very wicked man can cause to take place among the children of men" (Alma 46:9).

At the other end of the spectrum stands Moroni, an individual bulwark standing firm against the tide of wickedness. Others might have been overwhelmed by the fierceness of the battle, the swelling ranks of the enemy, or the recurring national domestic disputes among the Nephites. But rather than numbing Moroni into depression or paralysis, these challenges spurred him into action. And Moroni's conviction and character clearly rallied and lifted others as well, ultimately leading to success in battle. Hence Mormon's praise of this remarkable young military leader, for whom he presumably named his own son: "Yea, verily, verily I say unto you, if all men had been, and were, and ever would be, like unto Moroni, behold, the very powers of hell would have been shaken forever; yea, the devil would never have power over the hearts of the children of men" (Alma 48:17).

Two examples from my life remind me just how much difference one individual can make, even in very small things. I recall sitting in a stake conference while in college, when a member of the stake presidency suggested that all of the residents of our student apartments should eat at least one meal a day together. If there was a busier group of guys living together on campus, I hadn't met them, and coordinating our schedules so that we could eat one meal a day together seemed almost certainly impossible. I was about to lean over to my best friend and roommate to whisper something about this speaker being out of touch with reality, when Greg leaned over to me first and said, "I guess it'll have to be breakfast."

And breakfast it was. With that single comment, Greg nipped my cynicism in the bud and triggered a new apartment tradition: everyone took their turn making breakfast, and six days a week we ate better breakfasts than we'd ever eaten in college. And the counselor in the stake presidency was right: eating together daily really did improve our apartment unity. Greg's response to the counsel of this priesthood leader had made all the difference.

The second example involves an Orthodox Jewish friend of mine who attended a liberal arts college in California that was liberal in lifestyle and not just principle. His first year there, he was shocked when a resident assistant met with a group of new students and passed around a joint of marijuana. My friend was the last one in the circle—and the only one not to follow the RA's example of taking a puff. The next year my friend lived in the same place, so he decided to try an experiment. He sat next to the RA, who once again passed around a joint to the circle made up largely of freshman students. But this time my friend was the first one to get the joint, and he passed it on without taking a puff. Emboldened by my friend's example, no one else took a puff either.

Whether we want them to or not, our attitudes, actions, and character can have profound influences on others. On the one hand, when we choose to compromise standards or murmur against the Lord's anointed, others often follow our lead—to their spiritual detriment. Conversely, when we hold strong and stand for righteousness, our example often provides others with the courage they need to join in the cause. Whether for good or for evil, Moroni and Amalickiah remind us of the power of one—the power each individual has to make a difference.

Like the Nephites in Captain Moroni's day, as members of the Church, we find ourselves fighting against a large and formidable enemy that has as its goal our spiritual destruction. In a worldwide leadership training meeting in 2004, President Gordon B. Hinckley addressed our need to stand strong and overcome any fear:

> No one need tell you that we are living in a very difficult season in the history of the world. Standards are dropping everywhere. Nothing seems to be sacred any more. . . .
>
> . . . I do not know that things were worse in the times of Sodom and Gomorrah. . . .
>
> In the Church we are working very hard to stem the tide of this evil. But it is an uphill battle, and we sometimes wonder if we are making any headway. But we are succeeding in a substantial way. . . .
>
> We must not give up. We must not become discouraged. We must never surrender to the forces of evil. We can and must maintain the standards for which this Church has stood since it was organized. There is a better way than the way of the world. If it means standing alone, then we must do it.[3]

And when we muster the courage to stand strong in the face of opposition, we may be surprised how many other good people will follow our lead.

DEVILISH TACTICS

In his unyielding pursuit of power, Amalickiah also illustrated a number of tactics the adversary uses in his own never-ending quest for power over us:

Making house calls. Once he defected to the Lamanites, Amalickiah quickly drew the assignment of reining in those troops who refused to go to war against the Nephites (see Alma 47:3), such as those led by Lehonti. Although he was a violent man quite capable of commanding his followers to engage in outright war, Amalickiah sensed when trickery would be more effective than brute force. Thus, rather than attack Lehonti openly, Amalickiah sought to strike a deal with him secretly, pretending to defect to the dissidents Lehonti led (see Alma 47:8). Amalickiah's first choice was for the dissident Lamanite general to meet Amalickiah on Amalickiah's territory (see Alma 47:10–11), but when the general refused, Amalickiah did not give up. "And it came to pass that when Amalickiah found that he could not get Lehonti to come down off from the mount, he went up into the mount, nearly to Lehonti's camp" (Alma 47:12). Amalickiah's willingness to make a "house call" did the trick, and Lehonti soon naively agreed to Amalickiah's secret deal, which cost Lehonti his life.

In our day, too, Satan does all he can to lower the barriers of entry to sin. If we decline to visit him on his turf, he is quick to visit us on ours. It is no longer enough to refuse to frequent places of obvious temptation. The adversary now has the ability to bring pornography, lewd humor, spirit-numbing music, and graphic depictions of violence into our homes. Just thirty or forty years ago, those wishing to view pornographic films had to risk the embarrassment of being seen in public at adult theaters to consume their product. Now, executives of the "adult entertainment" industry gloat over the fact that they are able to deliver their product directly to people's homes. If we are to avoid falling as did Lehonti, we must not only decline Satan's invitation to come out to meet him, but we must also not open the door to our homes when the adversary knocks.

Flattery. Like Sherem (see Jacob 7:4), Amalickiah adeptly used flattery as a ploy. Those who supported Amalickiah's failed attempt to become king of the Nephites "had been led by the flatteries of Amalickiah, that if they would support him and establish him to be their king that he would make them rulers over the people" (Alma 46:5). A generation later, the head of the Gadianton robbers, Giddianhi, employed similar tactics in trying to persuade Lachoneus, the leader of the Nephites, to capitulate. He first complimented Lachoneus, giving him "exceedingly great praise because of [his] firmness" (3 Nephi 3:2). Giddianhi further promised Lachoneus that if the Nephites would "yield yourselves up unto us" they would become "not our slaves, but our brethren and partners of all our substance" (3 Nephi 3:7). Lachoneus undoubtedly perceived not only the moral bankruptcy of Giddianhi's proposal, but also its implausibility: if all the bankers quit to become bank robbers, there would be no banks left to rob.

Satan similarly appeals to our vanity in trying to convince us to throw our support to him. He uses flattery in a variety of ways, from filling us with pride about our perceived strengths (see, for example, Jacob 2:13) to enticing us to spend too much time doing things that would be fine in moderation—thus neglecting more important matters. He may also try to sway us from our priorities with promises of power—raises, awards, promotions, and other future payoffs.[4] In sum, Satan's strategy today is the same as it was in Amalickiah and Giddianhi's day—to buy off those who should be fighting against him by whispering to us that there's something in it for us if we abandon the cause or, at least, postpone the fight for a while. Temptations that would otherwise be transparent (for example, "We'll give you a $20,000 raise, but you'll be away from home three nights a week") become much more seductive when cloaked in flattery (for example, "You've got great potential, and this position shows that top management has real confidence in you").

Selling short. Amalickiah's enticements included more than just flattery. His proposition to Lehonti was straightforward and alluring:

Amalickiah would allow his men to be surrounded and conquered by Lehonti's army, if Lehonti would simply make Amalickiah second in command (see Alma 47:13). Lehonti would have then commanded the largest Lamanite army, if not the entire army, and would thus, in effect, become the ruler of the Lamanites. Overnight, he would go from being a rebel military leader to the man who would be king—all for the mere price of appointing Amalickiah his chief deputy. If all this seemed too good to be true, it was. Ultimately, Lehonti sold out his men and his honor for the privilege of presiding over a bigger army for what may have been just a few days.[5]

The adversary rarely approaches us empty-handed in his attempts to lure us away from our principled positions. Instead, his compromises and deals often feature promises of greater wealth, power, prestige, and security. Indeed, the young man who chooses to work full time instead of serve a mission will undoubtedly be able to drive a nicer car than his missionary friends. The salesman who fudges the truth may well outperform his peers in the short run. Parents who work beyond what is necessary to meet their family's needs may well be able to provide themselves and their children with some of life's luxuries. But in the final analysis, all who succumb to Satan's enticing offers will discover they have been doing business with a moral loan shark, who sells short-term pleasure with a hidden price tag of long-term pain.

Subtle death. Mormon prefaces the story of Amalickiah's rise to power among the Lamanites by noting that he was "a very subtle man to do evil" (Alma 47:4). Having fooled Lehonti into dropping his guard, Amalickiah completed his coup by having one of his trusted servants administer poison to the unsuspecting rebel general—not with one large dose, which Lehonti might have detected and rejected, but "by degrees" (Alma 47:18). So, too, the adversary usually seeks to bring about our spiritual death not with sudden, single-shot injections of temptation, but with such gradual doses of wickedness that our decline is almost imperceptible, until "he bindeth [us] with his strong cords forever" (2 Nephi 26:22).

Hired guns. Interestingly, in the case of both Lehonti (see Alma 47:14) and the Lamanite king (see Alma 47:22–24), Amalickiah delegated the actual act of murder to trusted servants. Perhaps the Lamanite king and Lehonti were less vigilant in dealing with Amalickiah's servants than they would have been had Amalickiah himself approached them. Moreover, after the dirty work had been done, Amalickiah was able to feign surprise and avoid any blame for the assassination he had ordered (see Alma 47:27).

Satan often employs others to make his arguments and commit the acts that spiritually destroy the unwary. Indeed, given his lack of a body, he and his minions appear to be somewhat dependent on enlisting the help of mortals. Alma the Younger's pre-conversion speeches, for example, gave "a chance for the enemy of God to exercise his power over" the people (Mosiah 27:9). Were it possible for the devil himself to approach us with temptation, how much less receptive and more vigilant would we be? Amalickiah's use of assassins reminds us that we must be vigilant against those whose arguments and activities may provide a disguise for the adversary in his attempts to exercise his power over us and bring about our spiritual demise.

FIGHTING FOR OUR FAMILIES

When reading the Book of Mormon as a young man with some pacifistic leanings, I was thrilled by the courageous stand for non-violence taken by the people of Anti-Nephi-Lehi in Alma 24. But my hopes of using the Book of Mormon to support an argument for universal pacificism were dashed when I reached Alma 43, where the

Lord makes it clear that the Ammonites' circumstances were the exception, not the rule. In fact, in Alma 43:46–47, the Lord not only permits but commands those engaged in righteous causes to defend themselves and their families with force, if necessary.

To be sure, there are some important limitations and cautions about not being guilty of the first or second offense.[6] With those caveats in place, however, the Lord uses *thou shalt* language to describe the Nephites' obligation to protect themselves: "Ye shall defend your families even unto bloodshed" (Alma 43:47). This commandment was not just a green light for the Nephites to vent their anger on their enemies. Instead, the Lord's directive was an order to the troops to spare nothing—including their own lives—in their efforts to protect their families.

Such a command was no small order. Not only did physical battle require the Nephites to risk their own lives, but it often involved the taking of others'. As Nephi's experience with Laban reminds us, even justifiable killing does not come easily to the righteous. Mormon later observes that those who carried out the Lord's order to defend their families unto bloodshed "were sorry to take up arms against the Lamanites, because they did not delight in the shedding of blood; yea, and this was not all—they were sorry to be the means of sending so many of their brethren out of this world into an eternal world, unprepared to meet their God" (Alma 48:23).

Most of us would not shirk from the task of defending our families if they were in physical danger—even giving up our own lives, if necessary. Yet are we as quick to make the less obvious sacrifices necessary to protect our families from spiritual dangers? Elder Neal A. Maxwell wondered, "Given the gravity of current conditions, would parents be willing to give up just one outside thing, giving that time and talent instead to the family? Parents and grandparents, please scrutinize your schedules and priorities in order to ensure that life's prime relationships get more prime time!"[7] Bishop H. David Burton further elaborated on the kinds of sacrifices parents need to make in our day: "Effective family leadership requires both quantity and quality time. . . . If giving your family quantity time means focusing less on providing the 'wants' in life or putting aside nonfamily involvement with fishing poles, golf clubs, boats, trips, and so on, those things should be done immediately."[8] Or perhaps protecting our families in our day requires us to give up certain career options so that we can be in our homes with our children, or certain entertainment choices so that the Spirit can be in our homes with our children. Just as the Nephites were required to defend their families from physical danger at great personal sacrifice, we are required to defend our families from spiritual danger at great personal sacrifice.

SHORING UP WEAKNESSES

With Amalickiah on the Lamanite throne, Moroni realized he faced an enemy who knew his Nephite people's strengths and weaknesses well. Indeed, Amalickiah had appointed former Nephites as his chief captains, "they being the most acquainted with the strength of the Nephites, and their places of resort, and the weakest parts of their cities" (Alma 48:5). Thus, Moroni began erecting forts and "throwing up banks of earth round about to enclose his armies, and also building walls of stone to encircle them about, round about their cities and the borders of their lands" (Alma 48:8). Moroni paid particular attention to his "weakest fortifications" (Alma 48:9).

As expected, the Lamanites under Amalickiah's command began their attacks at a city that "they supposed . . . would again become an easy prey for them" (Alma 49:3). Their hopes of an easy victory were dashed, however, because "the Nephites had dug up a ridge of earth round about them, which was so high that the Lamanites could not cast their stones and their arrows at them that they might take effect" (Alma 49:4). After being rebuffed in their first foray into the Nephite lands, the Lamanites then proceeded to the next weakest city, which to their disappointment, "had now, by the means of Moroni, become strong" (Alma 49:14). Mormon then observes: "Thus the Nephites had all power over their enemies" (Alma 49:23).

We, too, face an adversary who knows our strengths and weaknesses well. Thus, Elder David E. Sorensen suggests we follow Moroni's example in our personal battle against sin: "To avoid such temptations, be like Captain Moroni of old; set up 'fortifications' to strengthen your places of weakness. Instead of building walls of 'timbers and dirt' to protect a vulnerable city, build 'fortifications' in the form of personal ground rules to protect your priceless virtue."[9] To do this, we must first recognize our weakness. When we manage to muster the humility necessary to see our weakness[10] and seek the Lord's help in shoring up our defenses, we then are positioned to experience the wonderful miracle of personal fortification described in Ether 12:27:

> And if men come unto me I will show unto them their weakness. I give unto men weakness that they may be humble; and my grace is sufficient for all men that humble themselves before me; for if they humble themselves before me, and have faith in me, then will I make weak things become strong unto them.

In addition to effecting in us a miraculous change of heart, when we seek the Lord's help He may prompt us to take tactical steps akin to the fortifications Moroni built. For example, Elder Sorensen suggests fathers who are protecting their families would be "wise to keep computers and televisions in the family room or other high-traffic areas in your home—not in children's bedrooms."[11] As a bishop, I often counseled those struggling with a particular kind of temptation to seek to know in prayer a few tactical and practical safeguards the Lord would have them implement in their lives to help fortify their weak places. I know one young couple who struggled with consumer debt created by impulse purchases. They felt that a credit card could be an asset in their family if used correctly, but they wanted to guard against the kind of spontaneous shopping that had gotten them in a hole, so they placed the card in a Ziploc bag full of water and put + it in the freezer. After that, they only used it to make a purchase that had been planned hours in advance—with enough time for the ice around the card to melt.

Because our Heavenly Father knows our strengths and weaknesses even better than the adversary, He is in a position to inspire us to take the steps that will enable us, like the Nephites under Moroni's leadership, to have power over all our enemies (see Alma 49:23).

THE CONSEQUENCES OF SIN

*If we focus solely on the telestial glory sinners eventually receive,
we overlook an important post-mortal fact: the road to the telestial kingdom
first takes a long, miserable detour through hell.*

H ere's a simple yet difficult question: Will our friends who end up in the telestial kingdom be happy? Is the telestial kingdom hell—full of torment and regret—or is it part of heaven? And if it's part of heaven, is my friend correct who said to someone who was essentially living "without God in the world" (Mosiah 27:31) that he would be perfectly happy where he ended up, since he wouldn't be comfortable in a higher degree of glory? Few questions generate more discussion and more disagreement in my classes than these. But for all of us who love and live among those whose lifestyles may qualify them for the telestial kingdom, getting the post-mortal story straight about this particular fact is more than just getting another answer right in a game of Celestial Pursuit.

The fact is that as Latter-day Saints, we know more about the long-term destiny of most tenants of hell than the Bible alone gives us. The news is remarkably good and merciful for those who fear hell truly has no end. Yet armed with this additional light and knowledge, as gospel students and teachers we may sometimes forget that the news is also quite bad for those who don't believe hell is real or who merely think it's the disappointment of getting a Hyundai when you could have gotten a Lexus. Indeed, when I ask my students what hell is, they frequently answer that it is essentially the regret those in the telestial kingdom will feel, knowing they have missed out on celestial glory.[1] But they rarely mention hell as described in the Book of Mormon or even the Doctrine and Covenants.

Regret will certainly be an element of eternal suffering, but Book of Mormon prophets teach us that hell is much worse and much more than this. If in our gospel study and teaching we fast forward past hell and skip straight to the telestial state of things at the end of the story, we risk missing a very important point made emphatically by the Lord and His prophets in the Book of Mormon: Hell is a very real and a very terrible experience that we want to avoid at all costs. Thus, it is important that we understand for ourselves, our loved ones, and our friends the dangers of dying without repenting. And to the extent that others "look upon [us] as a teacher, it must needs be expedient that [we] teach . . . the consequences of sin" (2 Nephi 9:48).

THE EMPHASIS ON HELL

Book of Mormon prophets invoke the concept of hell 58 times in their writings.[2] Christ used the word five times Himself during His post-mortal appearances to the descendants of Lehi. Old-fashioned and out of vogue as the concept may be today, the collective intent of these scriptural passages is unmistakable: to warn us about the miserable condition that awaits those who die in their sins. Without question, the Lord and these same prophets freely and often simultaneously reminded their listeners of eternal blessings that await the obedient. Yet under the appropriate circumstances, they saw some benefit in alluding to the eternal stick as well as the carrot. As an exasperated Enos explained about the "stiffnecked people" of his times:

And there was nothing save it was exceeding harshness, preaching and prophesying of wars, and contentions, and destructions, and continually reminding them of death, and the duration of eternity, and the judgments and the power of God, and all these things— stirring them up continually to keep them in the fear of the Lord. I say there was nothing short of these things, and exceedingly great plainness of speech, would keep them from going down speedily to destruction (Enos 1:23).

Book of Mormon prophets did not find it useful or appropriate to discuss hell in every sermon or setting. However, they were prompted to speak of hell graphically and frequently enough that we may wish to learn from both what and how they taught.

HELL ON EARTH

In the most immediate sense, several Book of Mormon passages suggest that some sinners experience a taste of hell in mortality. On his deathbed, for example, Lehi pleaded with Laman and Lemuel to "awake from a deep sleep, yea, even from the sleep of hell, and shake off the awful chains by which ye are bound" (2 Nephi 1:13). In referring to his own suffering following the angelic visitation, Alma the Younger states, "I did remember all my sins and iniquities, for which I was tormented with the pains of hell" (Alma 36:13). Speaking of the conversion of the forefathers of church members in Zarahemla, Alma taught that they had been "encircled about by the bands of death, and the chains of hell" (Alma 5:7). Similarly, when Zeezrom began to realize the enormity of the sins he had committed, "his soul began to be harrowed up under a consciousness of his own guilt; yea, he began to be encircled about by the pains of hell" (Alma 14:6). Thus, hell is not only a post-mortal place of punishment but also an agonizing mental state that can begin here in mortality.

SELF-IMPOSED PUNISHMENT

Zeezrom's suffering also underscores the fact that whether in this life or the next, the anguish of hell will, to some degree, be self-imposed. His soul was "harrowed up under a consciousness of his own guilt" (Alma 14:6). Similarly, Alma taught that those who endure the misery of hell will suffer under a sharpened awareness of our sins:

> For our words will condemn us, yea, all our works will condemn us; we shall not be found spotless; and our thoughts will also condemn us; and in this awful state we shall not dare to look up to our God; and we would fain be glad if we could command the rocks and the mountains to fall upon us to hide us from his presence (Alma 12:14).

Joseph Smith also taught that it was a "perfect knowledge of all our guilt" (2 Nephi 9:14) that is the primary source of hell's torment:

> A man is his own tormentor and his own condemner. Hence the saying, They shall go into the lake that burns with fire and brimstone. The torment of disappointment in the mind of man is as exquisite as a lake burning with fire and brimstone. I say, so is the torment of man.[3]

FACETS OF HELL

Book of Mormon prophets emphasize at least three aspects of hell: captivity, heat, and endlessness. Whether metaphorical, physical, or both, each of these conditions illustrates how dramatic the effects of impenitent sin are and will be.

Captivity. The Book of Mormon refers repeatedly to "the chains of hell":

- "they are taken captive by the devil, and led by his will down to destruction. Now this is what is meant by the chains of hell" (Alma 12:11);

- "the chains of hell . . . encircled them about" (Alma 5:9);
- "What is the cause of their being loosed from the bands of death, yea, and also the chains of hell?" (Alma 5:10);
- "And may the Lord grant unto you repentance, that ye may not bring down his wrath upon you, that ye may not be bound down by the chains of hell, that ye may not suffer the second death" (Alma 13:30);
- "Yea, we have reason to praise him forever, for he is the Most High God, and has loosed our brethren from the chains of hell" (Alma 26:14).

The message of these passages is unmistakable: those in hell have lost their freedom; they will be and will feel captive to the devil. Indeed, Alma teaches that those who "harden their hearts" to the extent that "they know nothing concerning his mysteries" will be "taken captive by the devil, and led by his will down to destruction" (Alma 12:11; cf. 1 Nephi 14:4). Nephi alluded to the subtle stratagems used by Satan and the scarcely noticeable incremental slide that leads into this bondage: "[T]he devil . . . leadeth them by the neck with a flaxen cord, until he bindeth them with his strong cords forever" (2 Nephi 26:22). In tragic irony, then, those who have praised freedom while pursuing the pleasures of this world will ultimately yearn for the spiritual liberty they have forfeited through disobedience.

Heat. When we think of hell, we almost always think of heat. To many, the characterization of hell as a lake of fire and brimstone is so extreme that in modern popular culture, hellfire is more likely to be the humorous backdrop for a sketch on a late-night comedy show than the subject of serious conversation. The Savior, however, was entirely serious when he warned that those who vilified their brothers in anger were "in danger of hell fire" (3 Nephi 12:22). Moroni similarly warned that those who condemned his writings were "in danger of hell fire" (Mormon 8:17). Nephi described the brightness of hell as "like unto the brightness of a flaming fire" (1 Nephi 15:30), while both he and his brother Jacob referred to hell as "that lake of fire and brimstone" (2 Nephi 9:19; 2 Nephi 28:23; Jacob 3:11). Jacob provides one of the most descriptive references in this regard: "[W]herefore, they who are filthy are the devil and his angels; and they shall go away into everlasting fire, prepared for them; and their torment is as a lake of fire and brimstone, whose flame ascendeth up forever and ever and has no end" (2 Nephi 9:16; cf. Mosiah 3:27, where King Benjamin describes sinners' torment "as a lake of fire and brimstone"; see also Alma 12:17).

Is this fire merely symbolic? The use of the word *as* by Jacob (2 Nephi 9:16), King Benjamin (Mosiah 3:27), and Alma (Alma 12:17) suggests it is. Yet those headed for hell should not breathe a huge sigh of relief simply because all this talk of fire and brimstone is probably figurative. Prophets and the Savior have presumably chosen this symbol consciously and carefully. It is no accident that it conveys the feeling of consuming, intense, and unbearable suffering. Perhaps the most telling adjective of all is Jacob's, who calls the flames of hell "unquenchable" (Jacob 6:10).[4] Because the Savior loves us, He has warned us through prophets that, in effect, if we do not repent while we have the chance, we will one day wish desperately but vainly for relief from the fiery torment our sins produce.

Endlessness. Book of Mormon prophets use a variety of expressions to teach us that the detour to hell is anything but short-lived:

- "that hell which hath no end" (1 Nephi 14:3);
- "a flaming fire, which ascendeth up unto God forever and ever, and hath no end" (1 Nephi 15:30);

- "I have feared, lest for the hardness of your hearts the Lord your God should come out in the fulness of his wrath upon you, that ye be cut off and destroyed forever" (2 Nephi 1:17);
- "hell, and that lake of fire and brimstone, which is endless torment" (2 Nephi 9:19);
- "even a lake of fire and brimstone, which is endless torment" (2 Nephi 28:23);
- "an everlasting hell" (Helaman 6:28);
- "the eternal gulf of misery and woe" (2 Nephi 1:13).

As we learn later from the Lord in Sections 19 and 76 of the Doctrine and Covenants (and as discussed further below), these references are not to be taken literally, except for the sons of perdition.[5] Yet as with the symbolism of fire, we may be missing the prophetic point of these phrases if we dismiss them too quickly as simply being synonyms for God's punishment. Alma the Younger provided an important insight into the intense nature of a sinner's suffering when he described his own three days' of anguish in these terms: "My soul was racked with eternal torment" (Mosiah 27:29). If three days of suffering seems eternal, a millennium of anguish would certainly seem to be never-ending.

WHO GOES THERE

One of the challenges with the term *hell* is that the scriptures use the term in many ways. In its broadest sense, hell refers to "an abode of departed spirits."[6] All those spirits who await the resurrection view the "long absence of their spirits from their bodies as a bondage" (D&C 138:50). Virtually every Book of Mormon reference to hell, however, is in the context of those who have consciously disobeyed God's laws. Thus, Book of Mormon prophets generally are not discussing hell in this broad sense.

In its narrowest sense, hell describes the condition of the sons of perdition, the devil, and his angels.[7] When Jacob refers to the "everlasting fire" prepared for "the devil and his angels" (2 Nephi 9:16), he is presumably using hell in this sense. As President Spencer W. Kimball has reminded us, eligibility for becoming a son of perdition "requires such knowledge that it is manifestly impossible for the rank and file to commit such a sin."[8]

Most Book of Mormon passages discussing hell fall between these extremes. They describe the anguished state of ordinary people who consciously sin against God and decline to repent of their sins in this life. According to the Bible Dictionary, when "the Book of Mormon speaks of spiritual death as hell (2 Ne. 9:10–12)," it refers to the "temporary abode in the spirit world of those who were disobedient in this mortal life."[9] In other words, Book of Mormon references to the miserable state of those in hell cannot be dismissed as applying merely to a few individuals destined to become sons of perdition. To the contrary, these passages contain valuable warnings and information for anyone tempted to choose to walk contrary to God's commandments in this life.

COMPLETING THE PICTURE

As this discussion of the Book of Mormon and hell demonstrates, Latter-day Saints believe in hell as a very real and vivid experience to be avoided at all costs. Without question, our view of hell is much more dismal than the view of those who believe in no hell at all or who believe only in a watered-down version of it. (Not surprisingly, surveys show that people are more likely to believe in heaven than in hell.) We understand that the willfully disobedient will be subject to the devil and will suffer miserably for a very long time.

Yet through latter-day revelation, we also understand that in the end, the Lord is marvelously merciful to all but the sons of perdition. It is true that those who end up in the telestial kingdom will initially be "thrust down to hell" and there be subject to the power of the devil (D&C 76:84–85). However, they will be redeemed at the last resurrection (i.e., the end of the Millennium; D&C 76:38, 85).[10] At that point, they become "heirs of salvation" (D&C 76:88), inhabitants of a kingdom whose glory "surpasses all understanding" (D&C 76:89). Thus, with the exception of those sons of perdition who suffer endlessly in outer darkness, we realize hell is a "temporary abode . . . between death and the resurrection, and persons who receive the telestial glory will abide there until the last resurrection."[11]

Elder Dallin H. Oaks summed up our belief in this way: "Like other Christians, we believe in a heaven or paradise and a hell following mortal life, but to us that two-part division of the righteous and the wicked is merely temporary, while the spirits of the dead await their resurrections and final judgments." Then, as Section 76 makes clear, "Even the wicked . . . will ultimately go to a marvelous—though lesser—kingdom of glory. All of that will occur because of God's love for his children and because of the atonement."[12]

How can this temporary nature of hell[13] be reconciled with the numerous Book of Mormon passages suggesting hell is eternal? First, as the Lord explained to Joseph Smith, phrases such as "endless torment," "eternal damnation," and "endless punishment" are essentially synonyms for divine punishment: "For, behold, I am endless, and the punishment which is given from my hand is endless punishment, for Endless is my name" (D&C 19:10; see also D&C 19:6–7, 11–12). Second, as Alma's three days of "eternal torment" (Mosiah 27:29)

THE CONSEQUENCES OF SIN

demonstrate, finite punishment can be so intense as to feel infinite to those who endure it. Thus, in addition to referring to God's punishment, Book of Mormon passages about the endless nature of hell may also be warning us about punishment that will feel as if it is eternal, even though, mercifully, it is not.

Finally, while latter-day revelation clarifies and in some cases perhaps even corrects[14] the impression conveyed by Book of Mormon prophets that hell will be endless, the gist of those divinely inspired ancient warnings is still invaluable and accurate. It is entirely possible that the Lord revealed to Book of Mormon prophets exactly what most of us need to know about hell. Indeed, for planning purposes, we would be much better off assuming hell is truly endless than in assuming sinners can quickly or easily[15] get out of hell on telestial parole.

THEREFORE, WHAT?

Hell is not a popular concept with those at greatest risk of becoming its future tenants. Nephi forewarned us that the temptation to gloss over hell or deny its existence is, ironically, an argument inspired by its founder: "And behold, others he flattereth away, and telleth them there is no hell; and he saith unto them: I am no devil, for there is none—and thus he whispereth in their ears, until he grasps them with his awful chains, from whence there is no deliverance" (2 Nephi 28:22). Nephi's sobering warning should remind us that we do no one any favors by pretending there are no terrible long-term consequences to sin, because such beliefs tend to lead to disobedience and spiritual captivity. Thus, in referring to a Book of Mormon passage about hell, President Marion G. Romney reminded us that if we are to defeat Satan, "we must understand and recognize the situation as it is. This is no time for Latter-day Saints to equivocate."[16]

Knowing that hell ultimately has an escape hatch to a kingdom of glory is certainly marvelous and merciful news. Yet in trumpeting that headline, there is danger that we will miss the meat of the story. In explaining to Joseph Smith that terms such as "endless torment" and "eternal damnation" were synonyms for divine punishment, the Lord provided an additional explanation of his purpose that we sometimes overlook: "Again, it is written *eternal damnation;* wherefore it is more express than other scriptures, that it might work upon the hearts of the children of men" (D&C 19:7; emphasis in original). Like Enos, who found it necessary at times to remind his people of "the duration of eternity" (Enos 1:23), the Lord inspired His prophets to speak of "eternal damnation" and "endless torment" by design. His intent was not to scare us needlessly but to provide merciful warnings so vivid and graphic that they would "work upon the hearts of the children of men" (D&C 19:7). Certainly, much, if not most, of our emphasis in our gospel study and teaching should be on the eternal and present benefits of living righteously.

We all have friends and loved ones who may be on the telestial track. As a practical matter, knowing just where that train will take them fundamentally affects how bold I'm inclined to be in trying to persuade them to change trains. While they may be quite happy once they arrive in the telestial kingdom, they certainly will not be happy during the torturous journey through hell. When I think of what President Harold B. Lee called "the torture chambers of . . . hell . . . ," which he assures us are "terrible indeed as the Lord has warned," I cannot bear the thought of my friends and loved ones there. As I take the Book of Mormon's teachings to heart, I am motivated to do all I can, as President Lee challenged us, "to catch people on the way down before they reach that kind of a goal."[17]

THEREFORE, WHAT?

*Christ is the answer to many critical questions in the
Book of Mormon—and in our lives.*

Two LDS roommates and I once shared an apartment with Ahmed, a remarkable young man from Morocco. When Ahmed arrived, we told him that we lived the United Order in our apartment, which wasn't technically true, but it did capture the spirit of things. Of course, to Ahmed, it meant nothing. But even in his ignorance, Ahmed was more than willing to go along. "Wonderful," he replied. "And what is United Order?"

"We share everything we have," we simplified.

"Wonderful," he agreed with a smile. And it did turn out pretty well for him, since his luggage had gotten lost and he was my size. I gladly shared my clothes with him that first week, and he shared every meal he cooked with us. Over time, as we got to know Ahmed better, we also began to share thoughts about our respective religions. Soon, Ahmed was attending church with us and taking the missionary discussions.

Ahmed was astonishing. He prayed several times each day, and not just in some perfunctory way. Frankly, as we talked about how he approached prayer, I felt ashamed and inspired to improve the quality of my own prayers. Ahmed also essentially lived the Word of Wisdom and the law of chastity already—two things I had rarely found in combination among the many Germans I had taught as a missionary. Moreover, unlike most of my Christian friends outside the Church, he had no objection to the idea of continuing revelation. In fact, one Sunday when the Gospel Essentials teacher had passed out a sheet with pictures of all the prophets of the Church in this dispensation, Ahmed stopped us as we left church. "I have forgotten the pictures of the prophets. I must go back to get the pictures of the prophets."

We were delighted and excited as Ahmed progressed in his study of the restored gospel. The only hitch in all the discussions was his attitude toward Jesus Christ. Ahmed was very diplomatic and respectful. He had no objection to Jesus, he said. He may have even been a great teacher, a prophet perhaps. But Ahmed could not understand why we made such a big deal about Jesus and why we insisted he was the Son of God. After all, thousands of people had been crucified.

Ahmed had already easily cleared the most difficult behavioral hurdles that tripped up most of our German investigators. *If only we can get over this one last little hurdle of belief in Jesus Christ,* I found myself thinking—as if belief in Jesus were just another item on the checklist for a baptismal interview.

Could I have looked beyond the mark much farther? Like Ahmed, millions of good people honor God to the best of their ability, given the light and knowledge they have received, without knowing about or believing in Christ. My point is not that these people are foolish, but that I was foolish. Jesus Christ is not just another hurdle to be cleared on the path home to our Heavenly Father; He is the only way home to our Heavenly Father.

If there is a single motif running throughout the Book of Mormon, it is the reality of Jesus Christ and His centrality to the Father's merciful plan. Yet in addition to the most prominently displayed portraits of the Savior in this vast scriptural mansion, careful scrutiny reveals the Savior in some paintings and rooms where He is often overlooked. Elder Neal A. Maxwell taught that there "are panels inlaid with incredible insights, particularly insights about the great question"[1]— namely, "whether there is really a redeeming Christ" (Alma 34:5–6).[2] Indeed, "to answer affirmatively the great question is the very reason why the Book of Mormon and all Restoration scriptures were brought forth."[3] Not surprisingly, then, a thorough search reveals that the answer to so many critical questions in the Book of Mormon—as in our lives—is Jesus Christ.

PLANT THIS WORD

After listening to Alma's profound sermon on faith, his Zoramite listeners had a simple set of questions for Alma: Should they believe in one God, that they might obtain the fruit? How should they plant the seed or the word that Alma said they should plant in their hearts? How should they begin to exercise their faith (see Alma 33:1)? Woven throughout their explicit questions is this implicit query: Just what is this *word* that we're supposed to plant?

Initially, Alma doesn't address their question at all. Instead, he gently chides his listeners for supposing they could not worship God because they had been cast out of their synagogues (see Alma 32:5). If they believe such a thing, Alma notes, they obviously do not understand the real meaning of the scriptures (see Alma 32:10). Much like the Savior in John 5, Alma then exhorts his listeners to "search the scriptures"—not because the scriptures are the object of our worship themselves, but because they point us to the true object of our worship. "Search the scriptures," Jesus challenged the incredulous Jewish leaders, "for in them ye think ye have eternal life: and they are they which testify of me" (John 5:39).

Alma then proceeds to debunk the notion that worship can only occur in official places of worship—and to reveal simultaneously the object of our faith. To prove his point, Alma provides a list of unofficial places where the brass plates' prophet Zenos successfully worshipped: the wilderness, his field, his house, his closet, and—closest to home for the poor of Ammonihah—when he was "cast out and . . . despised by [his] enemies" (Alma 33:4–10). Wherever he prays, however different the places, Zenos expresses thanks for God's mercy. In fact, five times in these verses Zenos rejoices that God has been merciful to him. As Zenos and Alma elaborate on how God has been merciful, they begin to answer the question asked by the people in Alma 33:1.

Noting that his prayers have been heard, Zenos acknowledges the reason for such a blessing: "It is because of thy Son that thou hast been thus merciful unto me, . . . for thou hast turned thy judgments away from me, because of thy Son" (Alma 33:11). Alma underscores the importance of this particular point by asking his listeners if they really believe the scriptures (Alma 33:12). If so, he teaches, then they must believe what Zenos taught them—that it is because of the Son that the Father turns away His judgments (Alma 33:13). For a second witness, Alma then turns to Zenock, in a scripture that I wish were much more familiar to us than it is: "Thou art angry, O Lord, with this people, because they will not understand thy mercies which thou hast bestowed upon them because of thy Son" (Alma 33:16). Zenock's ancient Israelite listeners simply didn't get the Atonement. They failed to understand whom the object of their faith should be or, in the words of Nephi, "to what source they might look for a remission of their sins" (2 Nephi 25:26).

For a final witness, Alma turns to Moses (see Alma 33:19)—much as the Savior later would during his ministry in Judea (see John

5:45–47). Reminding us all how Moses held up the brass serpent in the wilderness as a type, Alma identifies a major obstacle to exercising faith in Christ both in Moses' day and in ours: finding it difficult to believe that He can heal us. "Now the reason they would not look," explains Alma of those who perished in the wilderness from snake bites, "is because they did not believe it would heal them" (Alma 33:20).

To be healed spiritually, Alma taught his listeners, they needed to exercise faith in their Redeemer, of whom the brass serpent was a type: "Cast about your eyes and begin to believe in the Son of God, that he will come to redeem his people, and that he shall suffer and die to atone for their sins" (Alma 33:22). Alma now ties together the elements of his answer to make it clear that he has actually been laying the groundwork to answer the original question about planting the seed or the word. "And now, my brethren, I desire that ye shall plant this word in your hearts"—referring to the Redeemer described in the previous verse—"and as it beginneth to swell even so nourish it by your faith" (Alma 33:23). In other words, Jesus Christ is the word or the seed, and when we exercise faith in him we nourish the seed so that it will grow and fill our hearts with "the joy of [God's] Son" (Alma 33:23). In short, Alma's challenge to his listeners and to us is to plant the Word—to believe the Savior when He promises He will heal us if we but return unto Him and repent of our sins (see 3 Nephi 9:13). Or as Amulek summarized his companion's teaching, Alma "proved . . . that the word is in Christ unto salvation" (Alma 34:6).

REDEMPTION COMETH THROUGH CHRIST

At the outset of Abinadi's "trial," King Noah's kangaroo court of priests asks Abinadi questions with very different motives than did Alma's listeners in Alma 32 and 33: these priests were fishing for some reason to execute this religious rebel who threatened to undermine their power (see Mosiah 12:19). One priest posits what was undoubtedly intended to be more of a challenge than an inquiry after truth: What does Isaiah mean when he praises the feet of those who bring "good tidings" (Mosiah 12:20–21)? Or when he prophesies that the Lord will "bring again Zion" and the restored people should "break forth into joy" after the Lord had "made bare his holy arm" (Mosiah 12:22–24)?

Perhaps this line of questioning was more of a rebuke than a riddle. Abinadi's message was all gloom and doom, the priest may have been implying, while true prophets brought good news. Abinadi accused Noah's people of having turned away from God, when the priests' party line might have been that these people had valiantly and courageously returned to the land of their rightful inheritance—their Zion, in essence—and the Lord had vindicated the wisdom of their decision by making bare His arm and allowing them to prevail in battle. The people alleged that Abinadi had "prophesied in vain" (Mosiah 12:14), and if the priests could successfully paint Abinadi as a false prophet, the law of Moses would justify them in executing him (see Deuteronomy 18:20).[4]

Abinadi's response is so long—and our typical scripture study so compartmentalized by chapters—that it is easy to overlook the fact that the prophet spends the next few chapters laying the groundwork for the answer to their question. Initially, Abinadi chides these imposter priests for their lack of scriptural and spiritual understanding: "Are you priests, and pretend to teach this people, and to understand the spirit of prophesying, and yet desire to know of me what these things mean?" (Mosiah 12:25).

When Abinadi asks just what the priests have been teaching the people, anyway, their answer is simple: "We teach the law of Moses"

(Mosiah 12:28). This gives Abinadi all the opening he needs. Their pretended piety does not fool him for a moment, and he lets them know he is fully aware of their whoredoms and hypocrisy (see Mosiah 12:29). Abinadi then asks the most critical question in his sermon: "Doth salvation come by the law of Moses? What say ye?" (Mosiah 12:31). Revealing their ignorance, the priests insist that salvation does come by the law of Moses. That's an odd position, Abinadi seems to reply, given your complete failure to keep that law (see Mosiah 12:33–37).

Undoubtedly unaccustomed to hearing such withering criticism, King Noah decides it is time to fast forward to the execution: "Away with this fellow, and slay him; . . . for he is mad" (Mosiah 13:1). While we may have forgotten the priests' original question, Abinadi's rejoinder makes it clear that he has not—and that he realizes he has not yet answered it. "Touch me not, for God shall smite you if ye lay your hands upon me, for I have not delivered the message which the Lord sent me to deliver; *neither have I told you that which ye requested that I should tell*" (Mosiah 13:3; emphasis added). When the people are perceptive enough not to attempt to execute a man whose face is shining like Moses', Abinadi returns to his sermon, underscoring the irony of priests who believe salvation comes by a law they flaunt. "And now I read unto you the remainder of the commandments of God, for I perceive that they are not written in your hearts" (Mosiah 13:11). Abinadi wants them to understand that although their answer was inaccurate because it was incomplete, obedience to the law does play a critical role in salvation (see Mosiah 12:33).

Having established the importance of obedience—and the fact of the priests' disobedience—Abinadi moves closer to answering the original question. While "it is expedient that ye should keep the law of Moses as yet[,]" Abinadi instructs, "salvation doth not come by the law alone; and were it not for the atonement, which God himself shall make for the sins and iniquities of his people, . . . they must unavoidably perish, notwithstanding the law of Moses" (Mosiah 13:27–28). Like Nephi, Abinadi appears to delight "in proving unto [his] people that save Christ should come all men must perish" (2 Nephi 11:6), notwithstanding all the zeal in the world in keeping the law of Moses or any other set of commandments. To borrow the terms of the economist, obedience is necessary but not sufficient. In fact, the law of Moses—with all its performances and ordinances—was to serve only as "types of things to come" (Mosiah 13:30–31). Like Sherem and the chief scribes and Pharisees after them, King Noah's priests failed to see the messianic point of the law through the forest of the ritualistic trees: "For they understood not that there could not any man be saved except it were through the redemption of God" (Mosiah 13:32).

Indeed, had not the Messiah and real redemption been the very focal point of every real prophet throughout time? "Yea, and even all the prophets who have prophesied ever since the world began—have they not spoken more or less concerning these things?" (Mosiah 13:33). As Exhibit A in support of his contention, Abinadi then recites for the record Isaiah 53—perhaps the most powerful prophecy of the Messiah in the Old Testament, conveniently located just a few verses after the very passage about which the priests had asked Abinadi. The priests who insisted that salvation came through the law of Moses had undoubtedly forgotten that the very meaning of Isaiah's name—*the Lord is salvation*—contradicted them.[5]

In providing commentary on the meaning of Isaiah 53, Abinadi finally answers the priests' question about Isaiah 52. Isaiah had declared that when the Messiah offered up his soul as a sacrifice for sin, He would see His seed (see Mosiah 14:10). Just who are His seed? Surely His seed includes the prophets and "all those who have *hearkened* unto their words, and *believed* that the *Lord* would redeem his people" (Mosiah 15:11; emphasis added)—both points on which Noah's priests fell short. Real prophets are, indeed, "they who have published peace, who have brought good tidings of good, who have published salvation" (Mosiah 15:14). In fact, Abinadi points out, the scripture can be interpreted at an even deeper level, since Isaiah surely spoke not only of the prophetic messengers who carried the good news of the Messiah's gospel, but of the Prince of Peace himself: "For O how beautiful upon the mountains are the feet of him that bringeth good tidings, that is the founder of peace, yea, even the Lord, who has redeemed his people; yea, him who has granted salvation unto his people" (Mosiah 15:18).

Finally, Abinadi makes sure that Noah and his priests are clear on the fact that their temporary success over the Lamanites in reclaiming Lehi-Nephi is far from the kind of redemption of which Isaiah prophesied. Those who believe in the Christ's words and keep his commandments will be the ones "raised to dwell with God who has redeemed them" (Mosiah 15:23). By this point in Abinadi's defense sermon, it seems likely that at least some of Noah's priests had lost a bit of their nerve and trembled at this prophetic indictment: "But behold, and fear, and tremble before God, for ye ought to tremble; for the Lord redeemeth none such that rebel against him and die in their sins" (Mosiah 15:26). And what of the salvation of God to be seen by all the ends of the earth (see Mosiah 12:24)? Folks in Lehi-Nephi were absolutely fooling themselves if they believed their little military conquest constituted salvation or that they were headed for spiritual salvation: "For salvation cometh to none such" (Mosiah 15:27).

Stretching forth his hand as he finished his discourse with a crescendo, Abinadi warned of the eternal consequences of those who are not redeemed, who remain carnal and devilish (see Mosiah

16:1–3). In conclusion, Abinadi reminded these priests in general—and perhaps Alma in particular—that real prophets bring genuine good news in the form of Christ, the only One in and through whom they can be saved: "Therefore, if ye teach the law of Moses, also teach that it is a shadow of those things which are to come—Teach them that redemption cometh through Christ the Lord, who is the very Eternal Father" (Mosiah 16:14–15).

Inadvertently and implicitly, perhaps, the priest's smug question had required Abinadi to answer the "great question"—whether there really is a redeeming Christ. And once again, the prophetic answer was a resounding yes.

THE CONDESCENSION OF GOD

One final example of a question that is answered indirectly yet masterfully is found in Nephi's exchange with the Spirit of the Lord in 1 Nephi 11. Wanting to see and hear and know for himself the things his father had seen (see 1 Nephi 10:17), Nephi is caught away in the Spirit into a high mountain, where the Spirit asks his desire (see 1 Nephi 11:1–2). Nephi's response is succinct: he wants to see the things his father saw (see 1 Nephi 11:3). Lehi's dream, of course, was fraught with symbolism and vivid imagery, but the Spirit chooses one symbol above all others to measure Nephi's faith: "Believest thou that thy father saw the tree of which he hath spoken?" (1 Nephi 11:4).

Nephi assures the Spirit that he believes "all the words of [his] father" (1 Nephi 11:5). Although the Savior has not yet been mentioned, the Spirit nevertheless rejoices "because thou believest in the Son of the most high God" (1 Nephi 11:6). The Spirit then outlines the vision to follow: Nephi will see the tree his father saw, followed by the Son of God descending from heaven (see 1 Nephi 11:7). Upon seeing the tree that was "precious above all," Nephi asks to know its interpretation (1 Nephi 11:9, 11). The Spirit does not immediately answer Nephi's question, but instead reveals the entire Nativity to Nephi, followed by a probing question: "Knowest thou the condescension of God?" (1 Nephi 11:16).

Confident in his knowledge that God loves his children, Nephi is not afraid to admit that he does not know the answer to this particular question (see 1 Nephi 11:17). The Spirit then elaborates on the birth of the Son of God. When Nephi's gaze is fixed upon Mary with Jesus in her arms, the Spirit teaches with a statement and a question, enabling Nephi to make a connection for himself:[6] "Behold the Lamb of God, yea, even the Son of the Eternal Father! Knowest thou the meaning of the tree which thy father saw?" (1 Nephi 11:21).

In his reply, Nephi explains that the meaning of the tree is "the love of God"—a phrase that often constitutes the totality of our explanation for the interpretation of the tree (1 Nephi 11:22). In the context of the Spirit's entire answer, however, the tree represents not just the love of God in general, but the highest manifestation of the love of God—the condescension of God, or "the Redeemer of the world" (1 Nephi 11:26–27). As Elder Jeffrey R. Holland concludes, "The life, mission, and atonement of Christ are the ultimate manifestations of the Tree of Life, the fruit of the gospel, the love of God, which 'sheddeth itself abroad in the hearts of the children of men.'"[7]

Given this ultimate answer to Nephi's question, it is not surprising that the description of the fruit of the seed planted in Alma 32 mirrors the description of the fruit of the tree almost perfectly.[8] Lehi beheld that the fruit of the tree was "desirable to make one happy, . . . sweet, above all that I ever before tasted" and "white, to exceed all the whiteness that I had ever seen" (1 Nephi 8:10–11). Because it "filled his soul with exceedingly great joy," it was "desirable above all other fruit" (1 Nephi 8:12). Similarly, Alma promised those who planted the Savior in their lives and exercised faith in Him that they would pluck fruit "which is most precious, which is sweet above all that is sweet, and which is white above all that is white, yea, and pure above all that is pure; and ye shall feast upon this fruit even until ye are filled, that ye hunger not, neither shall ye thirst" (Alma 32:42; cf. John 6:35).

THEREFORE, WHAT?

The crux of the matter is Christ.

I remember coming to the realization as a full-time missionary that I didn't need the Atonement just a little bit to make up for a few "shortcomings" here and there; I needed it desperately if I had any hope of being saved. Belatedly, I had come to understand that if I ever knocked on the door of heaven with an attitude that I deserved to be there—somehow having earned a mansion through my obedience—that a trap door would open to allow me to fall to the place I truly deserved. If I have any hope (and I do) of ever entering into God's presence, it is because I can say, "I'm with Him"—"relying wholly upon the merits of him who is mighty to save" (2 Nephi 31:19).

The more time I spend exploring the Book of Mormon with the Spirit as my guide, the more I come to know the Savior and the sweetness of His saving doctrines. I have come to understand that He prepares us against the refining and redeeming afflictions of life and leads us to lands of promise with His incomparable light. He invites us to flee the things of this world so that we might become separate from sin and one with Him. His prophets remind us that by remembering God's merciful hand in our lives—particularly the mercy He extends to us through the Atonement of His Son—our hearts become more attuned to receiving the further gift of revelation.

The Book of Mormon teaches us how Christ not only enables our hearts to be cleansed but to be changed—and thus enabled to do far more good than natural men and women could ever do on their own. Such changed men and women then transcend lusts for the vain things of this world—realizing they cannot carry such riches with them—and set their hearts instead on the things of God. Book of Mormon prophets also remind us that even changed men and women would drift off course without continually holding fast to the word of God. Of course, the spiritual knowledge necessary to keep us on the course home to Heavenly Father will come not from study alone, but through the Spirit, as Alma demonstrated.

Those who diligently published the peace of the gospel of Christ in the Book of Mormon also teach us much about leadership and parenting through their examples. As they faithfully magnified their callings on small stages, they emulated the Good Shepherd, who is quick to leave the ninety-nine to find the one (see Luke 15:4, 10). They remind us of the privilege it is to serve as undershepherds to Him who saved our souls, with all the diligence, love, focus, haste, and appropriate boldness we can muster. When our hearts are filled with such commitment to the cause of Christ, we will find it easier to be like Pahoran when fellow servants in the kingdom occasionally rub us the wrong way.

Because Christ loves us, He has given us His word to show us "all things what [we] should do" (2 Nephi 32:3)—including how to stave off the fiery darts of the adversary and "divide asunder all the cunning and the snares and the wiles of the devil" (Helaman 3:29). Such divine guidance is an essential defense against the weapons of an adversary who is flexible, subtle, and persistent in his efforts to lead us away from the strait and narrow path. Equipped with covenants, faith, and knowledge of our enemy's tactics, we will be prepared to make sacrifices and make a stand against evil for ourselves and our families.

As we battle against evil, we will remember that the stakes are high and the consequences of losing are real. Yet we will find comfort in knowing that we need not fight the battle alone. Jesus Christ stands eager to assist us at every turn, particularly in our personal battles to overcome sin. Thus, Moroni concluded his record with this invitation:

> Yea, come unto Christ, and be perfected in him, and deny yourselves of all ungodliness; and if ye shall deny yourselves of all ungodliness, and love God with all your might, mind and strength, then is his grace sufficient for you, that by his grace ye may be perfect in Christ; and if by the grace of God ye are perfect in Christ, ye can in nowise deny the power of God (Moroni 10:32).

How merciful, indeed, the Lord has been in granting us the gift of the Book of Mormon: Another Testament of Jesus Christ—the answer to life's great questions.

NOTES

NOTES TO "INTRODUCTION"

1. Dallin H. Oaks, "Following the Pioneers," *Ensign,* November 1997, 72.

2. Oaks, "Following the Pioneers," 72.

3. Jeffrey R. Holland, "Teaching, Preaching, and Healing," *Ensign,* January 2003, 37.

4. Dallin H. Oaks, "Gospel Teaching," *Ensign,* November 1999, 80.

5. Boyd K. Packer, "Do Not Fear," *Ensign,* May 2004, 79; see also Boyd K. Packer, "The Standard of Truth Has Been Erected," *Ensign,* November 2003, 24; Oaks, "Gospel Teaching," 79; Boyd K. Packer, "Washed Clean," *Ensign,* May 1997, 9; Boyd K. Packer, "Little Children," *Ensign,* November 1986, 17.

6. "There are a thousand hacking at the branches of evil to one who is striking at the root" (Henry David Thoreau, *Walden* [New York: Penguin Books, 1983], 119).

7. Neal A. Maxwell, *The Neal A. Maxwell Quote Book,* edited by Cory H. Maxwell (Salt Lake City: Bookcraft, 1997), 33.

8. Jeffrey R. Holland, "A Teacher Come from God," *Ensign,* May 1998, 26.

9. Holland, "A Teacher Come from God," 26.

10. Packer, "Do Not Fear," 79.

NOTES TO "PREPARED AGAINST THE WINDS AND MOUNTAIN WAVES"

1. John H. Groberg, *In the Eye of the Storm* (Salt Lake City: Bookcraft, 1993), 198.

2. "Lindbergh Nightmare," *Time*, February 5, 1973, 35.

3. Dallin H. Oaks, "Adversity," *Ensign*, July 1998, 7.

4. Nephi had a role model of his own when it came to being grateful amidst afflictions. Driven from his homeland into the wilderness and facing an uncertain future, Lehi "built an altar of stones, and made an offering unto the Lord, and gave thanks unto the Lord our God" (1 Nephi 2:7).

5. Dallin H. Oaks, "Give Thanks in All Things," *Ensign*, May 2003, 96.

6. Alma taught members to be "full of patience and long-suffering" (Alma 7:23), just as he taught that the Savior was "full of patience, mercy, and long-suffering" (Alma 9:26). Amulek exhorted the Zoramites "unto faith and to patience" (Alma 34:3).

7. During the days of Alma the Younger, the people "bore with patience the persecution which was heaped upon them" (Alma 1:25). Alma had great joy in his son Shiblon because of his "patience and . . . long-suffering among the people of the Zoramites," where Shiblon was in bonds and was stoned but bore "all these things with patience because the Lord was with [him]" (Alma 38:3–4). Captain Moroni noted that Helaman's stripling warriors had "patience in their tribulations" (Alma 60:26).

8. It is interesting to note that four years of camping on the beach preceded the Lord's three-hour chastisement to the brother of Jared for failing to pray (Ether 2:13–14).

9. Neal A. Maxwell, "The Tugs and Pulls of the World," *Ensign*, November 2000, 36.

10. "Indeed, when we are unduly impatient with an omniscient God's timing, we really are suggesting that we know what is best" (Neal A. Maxwell, "Hope through the Atonement of Jesus Christ," *Ensign*, November 1998, 63).

NOTES TO "OUR LIGHT IN THE WILDERNESS"

1. For a much more comprehensive analysis of the exodus pattern in the Book of Mormon than I present here, see M. Catherine Thomas, "Types and Shadows of Deliverance in the Book of Mormon," in *Doctrines of the Book of Mormon: 1991 Sperry Symposium on the Book of Mormon* (Salt Lake City: Deseret Book, 1992), 182–93.

2. Robert E. Cheesman, quoted in Hugh Nibley, *Lehi in the Desert and The World of the Jaredites* (Salt Lake City: Bookcraft, 1952), 72–73.

3. "Joseph Smith's account got the turn exactly right and also the area of increased desolation and 'much affliction,' including the interesting detail that the emigrants lived on raw meat, not being allowed 'much fire,' in this the one area of the trail where we now know they would have been in greatest danger of Bedouin raiders" (Eugene England, "Through the Arabian Desert to a Bountiful Land: Could Joseph Smith Have Known the Way?" in *Book of Mormon Authorship: New Light on Ancient Origins,* edited by Noel B. Reynolds [Provo: BYU Religious Studies Center, 1982], 152).

4. Terrence L. Szink, "To a Land of Promise," in *Studies in Scripture, Volume 7: 1 Nephi to Alma 29,* edited by Kent P. Jackson (Salt Lake City: Deseret Book, 1987), 66. The author goes on to acknowledge and briefly discuss the Lord's proffered explanation as an "additional reason" for the lack of fire.

5. That the ban was not complete gives credence to the notion that the prohibition on the use of fire may have been prompted in part by practical rather than purely symbolic reasons.

6. The fact that the scholarly yet speculative explanation about the need for limiting fire seems more broadly known than the Lord's explanation contained in the Book of Mormon itself suggests that we, too, may sometimes be guilty of "looking beyond the mark" (Jacob 4:14).

7. Jehovah similarly lit the way for the children of Israel as they departed the bondage of Egypt and took up their journey to their land of promise. "And the Lord went before them by day in a pillar of a cloud, to lead them the way: and by night in a pillar of fire, to give them light; to go by day and night" (Exodus 13:21).

8. "Both Babel and Babylon share the same Hebrew root word which means *confusion*" (Lee L. Donaldson, "The Plates of Ether and the Covenant of the Book of Mormon," in *Fourth Nephi through Moroni: From Zion to Destruction,* edited by Monte S. Nyman and Charles D. Tate Jr. [Provo, UT: Religious Studies Center, Brigham Young University, 1985], 76–77; emphasis in original).

9. "All Book of Mormon accounts of deliverance ultimately point the reader's mind to the greatest deliverance of all, the redemption of mankind from physical and spiritual death by the Lord Jesus Christ" (Thomas, "Types and Shadows of Deliverance in the Book of Mormon," 182).

10. See Moroni 7:16–17; D&C 84:45–46; 93:2.

NOTES TO "WHEN FLEEING IS HONORABLE"

1. The story of Lot's family is a marvelous Old Testament story illustrating this same principle. In the case of Lot's family, the temptations presented by Sodom and Gomorrah (including, presumably, the temptation to return), were so great that Lot and his family were commanded not only to flee "lest [they] be consumed in the iniquity of this city" (Genesis 19:15), but not to look back (Genesis 19:17).

2. Gordon B. Hinckley, "Thanks to the Lord for His Blessings," *Ensign,* May 1999, 88.

3. See Gordon B. Hinckley, "This Is the Work of the Master," *Ensign,* May 1995, 71.

4. Glenn L. Pace, "A Thousand Times," *Ensign,* November 1990, 10.

5. M. Russell Ballard, "The Doctrine of Inclusion," *Ensign,* November 2001, 37.

6. This is not to suggest that we should pray about whether it is permissible to live contrary to standards set by God's prophets. Instead, prayer serves to supplement the direction we receive from prophets in personal matters where they may not have provided definitive direction but have left us to exercise our discretion.

NOTES TO "RECOGNIZING GOD'S HAND SO WE CAN HEAR HIS VOICE"

1. For an eloquent elaboration of this phrase, see Elder David A. Bednar, "The Tender Mercies of the Lord," *Ensign,* May 2005, 99–102.

2. Several other Book of Mormon passages remind us of God's patient tenacity in calling after His children, even though we frequently do not heed the call. See, for example, 1 Nephi 21:15 ("For can a woman forget her sucking child, that she should not have compassion on the son of her womb? Yea, they may forget, yet will I not forget thee, O house of Israel"); Jacob 5:41 ("What more could I have done for my vineyard?"); 3 Nephi 10:15 ("how oft would I have gathered you as a hen gathereth her chickens, and ye would not").

3. Neal A. Maxwell, *Meek and Lowly* (Salt Lake City: Deseret Book, 1987), 59.

4. Melvin J. Ballard, *Crusader for Righteousness* (Salt Lake City: Bookcraft, 1966), 138.

NOTES TO "OF WHAT HAVE YE TO BOAST?"

1. Ben B. Banks, "This Road We Call Life," *Ensign*, May 2002, 42.

2. Dallin H. Oaks, "The Gospel in Our Lives," *Ensign*, May 2002, 35.

3. David A. Bednar, "In the Strength of the Lord," devotional address given at BYU-Idaho in Rexburg, Idaho, on January 8, 2002 (http://www.byui.edu/Presentations/Transcripts/Devotionals/2002_01_08_Bednar.htm).

4. Neal A. Maxwell, *One More Strain of Praise* (Salt Lake City: Deseret Book Co., 1999), 111.

5. James E. Faust, "The Weightier Matters of the Law: Judgment, Mercy, and Faith," *Ensign*, November 1997, 54.

6. *True to the Faith* (Salt Lake City: The Church of Jesus Christ of Latter-day Saints, 2004), 103.

NOTES TO "YOU CANNOT CARRY THEM WITH YOU"

1. The accounts of King Noah and the Gadianton robbers remind us that even the wicked may enjoy material prosperity. Thus, the trappings of prosperity are not reliable indicators of individual righteousness. Nor does poverty as to the things of this world necessarily demonstrate wickedness, as evidenced by John the Baptist and Joseph Smith.

2. Ezra Taft Benson, "The Book of Mormon–Keystone of our Religion," *Ensign*, November 1986, 6.

3. A search for *set* within five words of *heart* or *hearts* yields no results in the New Testament and 15 occurrences in the Old Testament. However, of those 15 passages, the phrase is used only once in the same context as it is used 14 times by Book of Mormon prophets, who always use the phrase (often in conjunction with riches or vain things) to denounce or describe those who aspire to materialism.

4. I do not mean to suggest that all nations or individuals enjoy unprecedented wealth. While some are experiencing remarkable abundance, others continue to languish in poverty.

5. C.S. Lewis, *Mere Christianity* (New York: Macmillan, 1952), 109–10. One of my colleagues points out to me that, ironically, we are also falling prey to pride when we take comparative pleasure in driving the cheapest car in the ward or being the most frugal.

6. Ezra Taft Benson, "Beware of Pride," *Ensign*, May 1989, 4.

7. C.S. Lewis, *The Screwtape Letters* (New York: HarperCollins, 2001), 155.

8. Henry David Thoreau, *Walden* (New York: Penguin Books, 1983), 80.

9. As Elder Joseph B. Wirthlin has explained, "And even if we are blessed enough to afford . . . luxury, we may be misdirecting resources that could be better used to build the kingdom of God or to feed and clothe our needy brothers and sisters" ("The Straight and Narrow Way," *Ensign,* November 1990, 65).

10. Dallin H. Oaks, "Our Strengths Can Become Our Downfall," *Ensign,* October 1994, 16.

11. The experience of the Saints in the early part of this dispensation and the corresponding revelations in the Doctrine and Covenants amply demonstrate this point. See, for example, D&C 42:29–39 (consecration required); D&C 104:53 (United Order dissolved); D&C 119:1–4 (Saints commanded to donate surplus property and pay tithing thereafter). For an excellent summary of these developments, which were more finely calibrated and nuanced than we sometimes recognize, see Blair Van Dyke, "Conquest of the Heart: Implementing the Law of Consecration in Missouri and Ohio," *Religious Educator* 3, no. 2 (2002): 45–65.

12. Exactly how we do that is beyond the scope of this chapter. None of the passages cited in this chapter suggests we must be indiscriminate or indifferent about how we achieve that goal, and living prophets have given us a tremendous amount of guidance about how to do so most effectively.

13. Spencer W. Kimball, *The Teachings of Spencer W. Kimball,* edited by Edward L. Kimball (Salt Lake City: Bookcraft, 1982), 354.

NOTES TO "SWIMMING WITHOUT LANES"

1. Surely the Lord could have prompted Nephi and his brothers to forgo the first two attempts and wait until Laban was drunk to retrieve the plates. But such a course of events would have eliminated at least two of Nephi's possible justifications: that Laban had "sought to take away" Nephi's life and that he "had taken away [their] property" (1 Nephi 4:11). Moreover, in allowing Nephi and his brothers to make their two unsuccessful pleas for the plates before guiding Nephi to the intoxicated Laban, the Lord was both fair and merciful toward Laban, who received not one but two chances to give up the plates of his own accord.

2. Perhaps this is the same reason Nephi was taught "in all the learning of [his] father," thus enabling him to "make a record in the language of [his] father" (1 Nephi 1:1–2).

3. The Lord emphasized the importance of the written word of God to Joseph Smith, Oliver Cowdery, and David Whitmer early in the Restoration: "I give unto you a commandment, that you rely upon the things which are written" (D&C 18:3).

4. Remembering all the commandments might be difficult in any dispensation, but this statement seems particularly true with the law of Moses and the 613 laws it encompasses. See Victor L. Ludlow, *Unlocking the Old Testament* (Salt Lake City: Deseret Book, 1981), 27.

5. Neal A. Maxwell, *Lord, Increase Our Faith* (Salt Lake City: Bookcraft, 1994), 103.

6. Ezra Taft Benson, "A New Witness for Christ," *Ensign,* November 1984, 6–7.

NOTES TO "NOT OF MYSELF BUT OF GOD"

1. See Alma 36, where Alma masterfully employs chiasmus, an ancient literary device, to symmetrically sharpen his narrative of his conversion story to make Christ the focal point.

2. Joseph Fielding Smith, *Doctrines of Salvation,* edited by Bruce R. McConkie (Salt Lake City: Bookcraft, 1954–56), 1:44; emphasis added.

3. Two marvelous biblical passages similarly convey the importance of learning spiritual truths through spiritual means. In 1 Corinthians 13:4–5, Paul reminds his readers why he taught them "not with enticing words of man's wisdom, but in demonstration of the Spirit and of power: That your faith should not stand in the wisdom of men, but in the power of God." Similarly, the Savior complimented Peter not only on his conviction that Jesus was the Christ, but on how Peter had obtained that conviction. "Blessed art thou, Simon Bar-jona: for flesh and blood hath not revealed it unto thee, but my Father which is in heaven" (Matthew 16:17).

4. Joseph stated that this was how 1 Corinthians 12:3 should be translated, which reads "no man can say that Jesus is the Lord, but by the Holy Ghost" in the King James Version. (See Joseph Smith, *Teachings of the Prophet Joseph Smith,* selected and arranged by Joseph Fielding Smith [Salt Lake City: Deseret Book, 1976], 223.)

5. Thus, the Lord chided Oliver Cowdery because he supposed "I would give it unto you, when you took no thought save it was to ask me" (D&C 9:7; see also D&C 88:118).

6. Dallin H. Oaks, "Teaching and Learning by the Spirit," *Ensign,* March 1997, 9. Elder Oaks then adds a cautionary caveat: "But if we are tied to them instead of to the Spirit of the Lord, we are not teaching the gospel in the Lord's way."

7. Henry B. Eyring, *To Draw Closer to God: A Collection of Discourses* (Salt Lake City: Deseret Book, 1997), 142.

8. Writing about one of the several symbolic meanings of the rock, Elder Bruce R. McConkie wrote, "Pure, perfect, personal revelation—this is the rock!" (Bruce R. McConkie, *Sermons and Writings of Bruce R. McConkie,* edited by Mark L. McConkie [Salt Lake City: Bookcraft, 1998], 115).

9. As Paul taught, "The natural man receiveth not the things of the Spirit of God: for they are foolishness unto him: neither can he know them, because they are spiritually discerned" (1 Corinthians 2:14).

NOTES TO "PLAYING TO SMALL CROWDS"

1. The people's cold reception to Lehi is, of course, a reflection on their wickedness, not on Lehi's abilities as a prophet.

2. It is possible that Abinadi's efforts laid the foundation or even resulted in the conversion of some of those who later joined Alma the Elder at the waters of Mormon; the record is silent on this point.

3. Ezra Taft Benson, "The Book of Mormon—Keystone of Our Religion," *Ensign,* November 1986, 6.

4. Given the similarities between King Mosiah's comments in Mosiah 29 and Alma's comments and conduct in Mosiah 23, it is likely that Alma's thinking about the dangers of monarchy influenced King Mosiah's decision to propose the fairly sweeping change from a monarchy to judgeships.

5. Gordon B. Hinckley, "An Ensign to the Nations, a Light to the World," *Ensign,* November 2003, 82.

6. Henry B. Eyring, "Rise to Your Call," *Ensign,* November 2002, 76.

7. I am indebted for this insight to Kim Beecher, a remarkable mother and teacher to her own children.

8. M. Russell Ballard, "The Atonement and Value of One Soul," *Ensign,* May 2004, 87; emphasis in original.

NOTES TO "THE GIFT OF A CALLING"

1. John Taylor, in *Journal of Discourses,* 26 vols. (London: Latter-day Saints' Book Depot, 1854–86), 20:23.

2. Dallin H. Oaks, "Why Do I Serve?" *Ensign,* November 1984, 14.

3. Dallin H. Oaks, "The Dedication of a Lifetime," CES Fireside for Young Adults, May 1, 2005.

NOTES TO "THE PAHORAN PRINCIPLE"

1. Neal A. Maxwell, *All These Things Shall Give Thee Experience* (Salt Lake City: Deseret Book, 1979), 119.

2. Mormon's decision to include this exchange between Moroni and Pahoran is impressive, given his obvious admiration for the Nephite general (see Alma 48:17). Since he was including only select materials in his abridged account, Mormon could have easily omitted this less than flattering episode from the life of a man whom he so admired. Instead, he had an attitude much like Elder Neal A. Maxwell's, who directed his biographer to resist the temptation to "dry all the human sweat off" because "it isn't that we're searching for weakness as much as we are for growth" (Neal A. Maxwell, in Bruce C. Hafen, *The Life of a Disciple: The Biography of Neal A. Maxwell* [Salt Lake City: Deseret Book, 2002], xv).

3. Neal A. Maxwell, *If Thou Endure It Well* (Salt Lake City: Bookcraft, 1996), 42.

4. Hugh Nibley speculates that Pahoran refrained from telling his generals about insurrections at home because he did not want to distract and discourage them from fighting enemies abroad: "Pahoran hadn't told him the bad news, lest it discourage the soldiers at the front" (Hugh Nibley, *Brother Brigham Challenges the Saints,* edited by Don E. Norton and Shirley S. Ricks [Salt Lake City: Deseret Book; and Provo, Utah: FARMS, 1994], 420).

5. Harold B. Lee, in Conference Report, April 1942, 95.

6. Maxwell, *All These Things Shall Give Thee Experience,* 119.

7. Maxwell, *If Thou Endure It Well,* 42.

8. Even after King Saul had turned against the Lord and sought David's life, David refused to kill Saul because "he is the anointed of the Lord" (1 Samuel 24:6).

NOTES TO "SATAN'S SLIPPERY SLOPES"

1. M. Russell Ballard, "Purity Precedes Power," *Ensign,* November 1990, 36.

2. Ezra Taft Benson, "The Book of Mormon Is the Word of God," *Ensign,* January 1988, 3.

3. James E. Faust, "'The Great Imitator,'" *Ensign,* November 1987, 34.

4. For someone who claimed to believe in a presumably all-powerful God, Sherem's arguments questioning prophecy are curiously contradictory to what should have been his core beliefs. Similarly, some in our day question the propriety of a belief in modern-day revelation, even as they stake their own claim to religious authority not on a chain of priesthood conferred from Christ but on personal inspiration calling them to represent Christ.

5. This belief also seems to have been a key and convenient tenet of the Lamanites' beliefs: "Notwithstanding they believed in a Great Spirit, they supposed that whatsoever they did was right" (Alma 18:5).

6. Billy Joel, "Only the Good Die Young," Columbia Records, 1977.

NOTES TO "SPIRITUAL COMBAT TRAINING"

1. I am certainly not the first person to suggest this approach to gleaning wisdom from the war chapters in the Book of Mormon. See, for example, Kathleen S. McConkie, "Defending against Evil," *Ensign,* January 1992, 19–21; and John Bytheway, *Righteous Warriors: Lessons from the War Chapters in the Book of Mormon* (Salt Lake City: Deseret Book, 2004).

2. I am indebted to my friend and colleague, Mark Beecher, for many of the insights contained in this section.

3. Gordon B. Hinckley, "Standing Strong and Immovable," Worldwide Leadership Training Meeting, January 10, 2004, 20.

4. For a wonderful discussion of how even our work and our hobbies may be among the things that pull us away from Heavenly Father, see Joseph B. Wirthlin, "'Follow Me,'" *Ensign,* May 2002, 15–17.

5. Alma 47 does not indicate exactly how long after Amalickiah's surrender Lehonti was assassinated, but from the flow of the narrative it seems likely that it was not long.

6. Note also the restraint shown by the righteous Nephite leader Gidgiddoni when the righteous Lamanites and Nephites were later besieged by the Gadianton robbers. The robbers had openly vowed to destroy the

people, who understandably pled with Gidgiddoni to go after the outlaws and "destroy them in their own lands" (3 Nephi 3:20). Gidgiddoni steadfastly refused to take such preemptive action: "The Lord forbid; for if we should go up against them the Lord would deliver us up into their hands; therefore we will prepare ourselves in the center of our lands, and we will gather all our armies together, and we will not go against them, but we will wait till they shall come against us; therefore as the Lord liveth, if we do this he will deliver them into our hands" (3 Nephi 3:21).

7. Neal A. Maxwell, "'Take Especial Care of Your Family,'" *Ensign,* May 1994, 90.

8. H. David Burton, "'I Will Go,'" *Ensign,* November 1995, 45.

9. David E. Sorensen, "You Can't Pet a Rattlesnake," *Ensign,* May 2001, 41.

10. Interestingly, the ability to see ourselves accurately—as the Lord sees us—is a characteristic of those who enjoy celestial glory: "They see as they are seen" (D&C 76:94).

11. Sorensen, "You Can't Pet a Rattlesnake," 41.

NOTES TO "THE CONSEQUENCES OF SIN"

1. There is a doctrinal basis for such comments. Joseph Smith said, "The great misery of departed spirits in the world of spirits, where they go after death, is to know that they came short of the glory that others enjoy and that they might have enjoyed themselves, and they are their own accusers" (*History of The Church of Jesus Christ of Latter-day Saints,* 7 vols., edited by B. H. Roberts, 2d ed. rev. [Salt Lake City: The Church of Jesus Christ of Latter-day Saints, 1932–51], 5:425). Elder John Widtsoe echoed these comments when he said that "hell is to find ourselves in an inferior position and conditions, and to know that we might have been, by our efforts, in a higher and more glorious place, had we exercised our free agency more vigorously for better things" (quoted in Alan K. Parrish, "Doctrine & Covenants 76 and the Visions of Resurrected Life in the Teachings of Elder John A. Widtsoe," in *Doctrines for Exaltation: The 1998 Sperry Symposium on the Doctrine and Covenants,* edited by Susan Easton Black [Salt Lake City: Deseret Book, 1989], 211–12).

2. See 1 Nephi 12:16; 14:3 (twice); 15:29, 35; 2 Nephi 1:13, 15; 4:32; 9:10, 12 (three times), 19, 26, 34, 36; 15:14; 24:9, 15; 26:10; 28:15, 21, 22, 23

(twice); 33:6; Jacob 3:11; 7:18; Alma 5:6, 7, 9, 10; 11:23; 12:11; 13:30; 14:6; 19:29; 26:13, 14; 30:60; 31:17; 36:13; 37:16; 48:17; 54:7, 11, 22; Helaman 6:28; 3 Nephi 11:39, 40; 12:22, 30; 18:13; Mormon 8:17; 9:4; Moroni 8:13, 14, 21.

3. Smith, *History of the Church,* 6:314.

4. Jacob's description brings to mind the Savior's parable of Lazarus, in which the rich man's greed leads him to hell. "Being in torments" (Luke 16:23), he begs in vain for a drop of water to quench his insatiable suffering and cool his tongue (Luke 16:24–26). Elder Bruce R. McConkie portrayed hell in this way: "Death can be comforting and sweet and precious or it can thrust upon us all the agonies and sulphurous burnings of an endless hell. And we—each of us individually—make the choice as to which it shall be" ("The Dead Who Die in the Lord," *Ensign,* November 1976, 106).

5. While hell continues for the sons of perdition after the resurrection, its venue apparently changes. "Hell in the spirit world will end when all people have been resurrected. Because of the atonement of Christ, there is an eventual release. (See 2 Ne. 9:6–12.) Those who remain 'filthy still' (the sons of perdition) will remain in hell, but it will be a place separate from the hell of the spirit world. (See D&C 76:43-49.)" (Dale C. Mouritsen, "The Spirit World, Our Next Home," *Ensign,* January 1977, 48).

6. Bible Dictionary, s.v. "Hell."

7. "The devil and his angels, including the sons of perdition, are assigned to a place spoken of as a lake of fire—a figure of eternal anguish. This condition is sometimes called hell in the scriptures" (Bible Dictionary, s.v. "Hell").

8. Spencer W. Kimball, *The Miracle of Forgiveness* (Salt Lake City: Bookcraft, 1969), 123. Whether Laman and Lemuel and Alma the Younger had sufficient light to become sons of perdition is unclear. It is possible that some verses involving such enlightened individuals who sin may also pertain to that hell which will host the sons of perdition.

9. Bible Dictionary, s.v. "Hell."

10. Elder James E. Talmage suggests that penitent sinners may be released from hell even sooner: "Hell is no place to which a vindictive judge sends prisoners to suffer and to be punished principally for his glory; but it is a place prepared for the teaching, the disciplining of those who failed to learn here upon the earth what they should have learned." Speaking of the label of hell as eternal punishment, Elder Talmage continues, "This does not mean

that the individual sufferer or sinner is to be . . . kept in hell longer than is necessary to bring him to a fitness for something better. When he reaches that stage the prison doors will open and there will be rejoicing among the hosts who welcome him into a better state" (in Conference Report, April 1930, 97).

11. Bible Dictionary, s.v. "Hell."

12. Dallin H. Oaks, "Apostasy and Restoration," *Ensign,* May 1995, 86, 87.

13. "Hell, then, is a temporary quarter of the spirit world where the wicked are restrained in order for justice to be served and to give them a chance to repent. The Lord's promise is that all who do repent will receive a kingdom of glory, according to his judgment of their works" (H. Donl Peterson, "I Have a Question," *Ensign,* April 1986, 37).

14. In Mosiah 16:11, for example, Abinadi refers to those who are evil being raised "to the resurrection of endless damnation, being delivered up to the devil," a sequence of events that does not seem to synchronize precisely with the more complete and more recent revelation of Doctrine and Covenants 76.

15. Nothing in Doctrine and Covenants 76 suggests that departure from hell will be either easy or quick. To the contrary, those destined for the telestial kingdom are described as those "who suffer the vengeance of eternal fire. These are they who are cast down to hell and suffer the wrath of Almighty God, until the fulness of times" (D&C 76:105–6), or, in other words, for at least the 1,000 years between the start of the Millennium and the last resurrection (see D&C 76:85).

16. Marion G. Romney, "Satan—The Great Deceiver," *Ensign,* June 1971, 36.

17. Harold B. Lee, "Priesthood Address," *Ensign,* January 1974, 101.

NOTES TO "THEREFORE, WHAT?"

1. Neal A. Maxwell, *Not My Will, But Thine* (Salt Lake City: Bookcraft, 1979), 33.

2. Maxwell, *Not My Will, But Thine,* 15.

3. Maxwell, *Not My Will, But Thine,* 17.

4. I am indebted to John W. Welch for shedding this light on the priests' possible motives in asking Abinadi about this particular passage of scripture,

as well as for pointing out how Abinadi answers the priests' original question.

5. I am indebted to John Bytheway for this insight.

6. Elder David A. Bednar has highlighted the way the Spirit teaches Nephi in 1 Nephi 11–14 as an example of how great teachers help their students learn by faith by giving them opportunities to participate in discovering insights. (See David A. Bednar, "Seek Learning by Faith," Address to Religious Educators, West Jordan, Utah, February 3, 2006, 3.)

7. Jeffrey R. Holland, *Christ and the New Covenant* (Salt Lake City: Deseret Book, 1997), 161.

8. Elder Holland points out this connection as well as the importance of Alma 33 and 34 in defining the word we are to plant (see Holland, *Christ and the New Covenant*, 169–70).

INDEX

Oaks, Dallin H.: on gospel teaching,
xi–xii; on our reaction to adversity,
5; on gratitude, 8; on Church
teachings, 38; on over-generosity,
59; on intellectual preparation for
testimony, 79, 180n6; on serving
because of love, 98; on messages
from leaders, 108–9; on heaven
and hell, 156
Obedience: benefits of, 37–39, 42; and
gratitude, 44–45; and prosperity,
47–48; unhesitating, 101–3;
progressive nature of, 126
Object lessons, 13–15
Ocean voyages, 2–4
Offense, not taking, 113–19

Pace, Glenn L., 23
Packer, Boyd K., xi, xii
Pahoran, 113–18, 181n2, 181n4
Patience: in times of trial, 8–9, 10,
174nn6–7, 174n10; of Pahoran,
118; of God, 176n2
Peter, 179n3
Peterson, H. Donl, 185n13
Philanthropy, 56–59, 178n9
Pluralistic societies, 22–26
Pondering: in Moroni's challenge,
29–31; mercy of the Lord, 30; the
Atonement, 31; and revelation, 32
Prayer: intensity of, 1; for the right
things, 6–7, 176n6; precision of,
13; of gratitude, 33, 162; and
revelation, 104–7; in secular life,
135
Preparation: for trials, 1–12; Jaredites',
for voyage, 2–4; vs. faith, 135–36
Pride, 51–54, 177n5
Promises, Satan's, 141–42
Prophetic counsel, 176n6
Prophets: following, 21–22; calling of
Book of Mormon, 101; response to,
107; message of, 164; doubting of,
182n4
Prosperity: spiritual risk of, 46; and
obedience, 47–48, 177n1; Mormon
and Moroni's perspective on,
48–50; dangers of, 50–51, 177n3;

in our day, 50–51, 177n4; and
pride, 51–54; as a goal, 54–56;
righteous uses of, 56–59, 61–64,
178n9; transitory nature of, 60–61

Rameumptom, 129
Regret, 148–49, 183n1
Religions, balance of relationships with
other, 23–25
Repentance, 39–42, 44
Respect, 24, 31–32
Revelation: being receptive to, 29,
32–33; and testimony, 80; and
prayer for others, 104–7; personal,
as rock, 180n8; as inconsistent
with world's beliefs, 182n4
Righteousness, 35–39, 47–49
Romney, Marion G., 157

Sacrifice, 103–4
Samuel the Lamanite, 107, 128
Sanctification, 22
Satan: tactics of, 123–32, 139–43;
flexibility of, 124–25; and hatred,
134; and hell, 151–52
Saul, 181n8
Scriptures: importance of, 67–74,
179n3; brass plates as, 68–69; and
Mulekites, 69–70; King Benjamin
understands importance of, 70–72;
studying, 71–74; and memory,
72–73; and recognizing God's
mercy, 73; as pointer to Jesus
Christ, 161–62; as education,
179n2
Service, 106–7
Sherem, 127, 182n4
Shiblon, 174n7
Sin, 146–47
Small plates of Nephi, 89–90
Smith, Joseph: on Holy Ghost as source
of testimony, 78, 179n4; on hell,
151; on misery of the dead, 183n1
Smith, Joseph Fielding, 77–78
Sons of perdition, 154, 155, 184n5,
184nn7–8
Sorensen, David E., 146–47
Spirit, 24–25, 186n6

ABOUT THE AUTHOR

Rob Eaton is a professor of religious education at BYU–Idaho and speaks regularly at BYU Education Week. He has also taught seminary and institute and served as a bishop in The Church of Jesus Christ of Latter-day Saints. A graduate of BYU and Stanford Law School, he has also worked as a research assistant for F.A.R.M.S., an attorney, and a corporate vice president prior to teaching religion full-time. He and his wife, Dianne, live in Rexburg, Idaho, and are the parents of four children.